Heartaches and Miracles

Greta Burroughs

cover art by Robert F. DeBurgh

Copyright © 2011 Greta Burroughs

All rights reserved.

ISBN: 1466217650
ISBN-13: 978-1466217652

DEDICATION

This book is dedicated to my husband, Bob who has faithfully stood by my side through all the relapses and remissions associated with my ITP. I could never ask for a better, more patient and loving caregiver. We were, still are and will always be a team. Together we have learned how precious life is and how to cope with any obstacle placed in our way.

This narrative is also dedicated to my parents, Vernon and Allison Wilson. They kept us in their thoughts and prayers, even though they were both suffering their own fights with cancer. Their positive attitude was an example for us to follow in our fight with ITP and their strong support never failed, no matter how sick they each became.

CONTENTS

	Foreword	i
	Introduction	iii
	Acknowledgements	v
1	Struck by Lightning	1
2	Five Days and Nights in PCU	10
3	Home Sweet Home	25
4	Relapse	39
5	Relapse Again and Again	60
6	What Do We Do Now	71
7	The Gift of Sight	83
8	Remission	95
	About the Author	107
	Other Books by Greta Burroughs	109
	Recommended Reading	111

FOREWORD

When Greta first came down with ITP, I had no idea just how serious this insidious disease could be. The reality of this ailment was brought home to me when she was first admitted to the hospital with a platelet count of only 2,000 and falling. In spite of my lay medical training and experience, first as an EMT in Vermont and later as a volunteer medical assistant at a bush hospital in Southwest Africa, I had no clear idea what was wrong with her and mistakenly thought the problem may have been Dengue Hemorrhagic Fever (DHF) or Rift Valley Fever, both with similar symptoms. What did not fit was the lack of a high fever, which is present in most of the tropical blood diseases.

The doctors at the hospital were also baffled as to the cause of her dropping platelet count, bruises, heavy bleeding and petechiae. Finally a hematologist was called in and he finally recognized what the cause of her symptoms was. I did not realize until later exactly how close I was to losing my beloved wife at that time.

From there it has been a battle for the last six years to find a treatment that would hold this disease at bay. There have been ups and downs, improvements and relapses, a true roller coaster ride of emotions on both our parts. I have been husband, nurse, caregiver and giver of strength, as well as housekeeper and chauffeur at times. All this I have done gladly and during these trying times have learned much about diseases of the immune system.

One thing I have learned is that much more research needs to be done in this area of medicine along with better training of doctors, general practitioners in particular, in recognition and treatment of autoimmune disorders.

I hope this book can become a beacon of hope to all sufferers of ITP and related disorders and the spark for more research, better medications with fewer side effects and finally, a cure.

Robert F. DeBurgh

INTRODUCTION

This is for everyone suffering with ITP, Immune (Idiopathic) Thrombocytopenic Purpura. Whether you have this blood disorder yourself or know of someone with ITP, hopefully, sharing my story with you will help you to understand this immune system disorder.

ITP is not easily diagnosed and occurs most of the time without warning. The indications such as unexplained bruising, bleeding or low platelet count can be caused by a number of different factors and diseases. ITP can be misdiagnosed and improperly treated by physicians who are not familiar with blood disorders and that can lead to serious consequences.

ITP also varies from patient to patient. Some have spontaneous remission while others like myself develop refractory ITP, which means the disease does not respond to standard treatments and more innovative measures have to be taken.

In all cases, the victims of this autoimmune disorder have to learn what ITP is and how it is treated. Luckily, I have a very patient hematologist who has been with us all through this ordeal, Dr. Renwick Goldberg from Coastal Cancer Center in Myrtle Beach, SC. He has calmed our fears, cheered our successes and been our guide on this very rocky road. He also allowed me to pick his brain for information while writing articles on autoimmune disorders and this book.

Before my diagnosis, I had never heard of ITP, but since then I have become aware that ITP is not as rare as I first thought. There have been friends and acquaintances of my family who have had this disorder, but such information was not made known to me until after my diagnosis.

I have also met people who work in stores or at the hospital that have or know of someone with ITP. I even had an email friend whom I have never met personally, but incidentally found out we share the same blood disease. We were corresponding about another matter when I mentioned my ITP and found out she had it too.

It is a small world when it comes to finding things I have in common with friends, acquaintances and even total strangers.

Come, be a part of my world while I share with you my story of my struggle with Immune Thrombocytopenic Purpura.

Greta

ACKNOWLEDGEMENTS

Through our internet search, we found a website hosted by the Scripps Institute, http://www.scripps.edu. Scripps has done extensive research on ITP led by Dr. Robert McMillan, a renowned authority on the subject. Dr. McMillan is now retired but has given me permission to use some of his research and information from the Scripps ITP website in this narrative.

I have also used information from AARDA (American Autoimmune Related Diseases Association, http://www.aarda.org. I interviewed Virginia Ladd, president and executive director of AARDA and she provided invaluable information on autoimmune disorders for this book and for various articles I have written on the subject.

PDSA (Platelet Disorder Support Association) http://www.pdsa.org specializes in ITP and has a website with current information concerning patient education, support services, public education as well as research and advocacy. They also have a forum where you can post questions and have discussions with other people with ITP.

Caroline Kruse, executive director of PDSA granted me permission to use material from the website. PDSA also has a toll free telephone number: 1- 87-PLATELET (877- 528-3538).

On the PDSA Facebook page, "ITPers" share experiences and it is a wonderful place to communicate with others sharing the same autoimmune disorder. I have included excerpts from my Facebook friends throughout the book, expressing their thoughts on ITP and the impact it has had on their lives.

I owe a big thank you to all these people and of course to Dr. Renwick Goldberg for his guidance; not only for his help in writing my book, but also for being our hematologist and friend during my ITP roller coaster ride.

1 STRUCK BY LIGHTNING

ITP makes dealing with everything a flip of the coin. The reaction may be nothing, or it could turn into a 1970's disaster film starring Charleton Heston. ITP is an adventure to say the least!

Tom Schilling - Greenville, IL

Friday, April 29, 2005

"But I don't feel sick. Why do I have to stay here in the hospital?" I stubbornly asked the emergency room doctor. He replied in an exasperated voice, "Because you are one sick chick. Your platelets are down to 2000. You are going upstairs to PCU and you are going to stay there until I say you can go home."

So was the beginning of my ordeal with ITP. I was so scared and confused. I had never been in a hospital as a patient before and did not think it was necessary then. What did it mean, "My platelets were down to 2000?" Why was I so tired? Why did I have all those bruises and what were those strange red dots all over my legs?

That was my 'Black Friday.' During the three to four weeks prior to my visit to the emergency room, I knew something was wrong but never dreamed it would turn out to be life-threatening. I had been through quite an ordeal trying to find the reason for the nonstop heavy, vaginal bleeding that had been plaguing me for over a month and was very frustrated with the lack of progress. I wanted answers and a way to put an end to it and believed it was my doctor's job to fix it.

The day prior to going to the hospital, I suffered through another nonproductive visit with an ob/gyn. After going through all types of poking and prodding, answering countless questions and submitting myself to endless tests, the results were supposed to be revealed to me.

"Your Pap smear is OK. Your biopsy is OK. Everything looks good, Greta. I think you are premenopausal and the Provera I prescribed should get your periods back under control. You are at the age when things like this happen. If the Provera doesn't help, we'll talk about alternative treatments we can try."

I was not satisfied. "How about doing some blood work. I feel really tired all the time and I've got all these bruises all over my arm. Could I be anemic from all the bleeding over the past few weeks?"

That was my fourth visit to Dr. Meyers and I was perplexed as to why she never did any blood work on the previous three visits. Probably being an ob/gyn, the good doctor assumed the ninety-nine out of a hundred cause for my prolonged bleeding was menopause. She did the routine gynecological tests to rule out other causes, such as cervical or uterine cancer, but never thought of checking for a blood disorder.

Early the next morning when the telephone rang, an excited voice from the clinic informed me, "You need to get to the hospital right now. We got the lab results from your blood work we did yesterday and there is a panic alert on your platelet levels. Come by our office and pick up some paperwork and go directly to the hospital and let them double-check our results in their lab. If the results are the same, you will need to go to the emergency room immediately."

That was not what I wanted to hear at seven o'clock in the morning. I had things to do, busy, busy, busy, every day there was so much to do. We had seven dogs I needed to walk, exercise and feed. The yard needed to be shoveled; seven big dogs eat lots of dog food. The house was a mess; dirty laundry was overflowing the hamper, there were end of the month bills to be sent out and groceries to be purchased. I did not have time to go to the hospital.

I told the nurse I would be down later in the afternoon. In return, I received a lecture on the seriousness of the situation and to get there as soon as possible, in other words, right now. After relaying the news to my husband, we scrubbed all the plans we had for the morning and went to the emergency room expecting to have the afternoon to complete all our work.

Actually the past year had been very hectic, so much to do and so little time. My husband, Bob had developed heart problems in May 2004, which resulted in three stents being surgically implanted in the arteries around his heart. That was stressful enough, but in addition, his career as a professional pilot came to an abrupt end due to the loss of his medical certificate, which meant our major source of income came to an abrupt end as well. Up until that time, we had been self-employed, working together and had everything pretty well under control. Twenty years earlier we had started our own business, teaching aviation ground schools and administering flight and written tests for the Federal Aviation Administration.

I was office manager and did all the paperwork, bookkeeping, scheduling, etc. and obtained my ground instructor rating so that I could help Bob teach the ground schools. I also became a designated written-test examiner administering the FAA written tests for all the pilot ratings, flight engineer and airplane mechanic certificates.

Bob became a designated pilot examiner for the Federal Aviation Administration. He tested student pilots for private pilot and more advanced ratings and issued pilot certificates to the applicants who passed the checkride. It was a very prestigious position recognizing the skill, knowledge and wisdom gained through all his years as a professional pilot and flight instructor. He was well respected by the aviation community and his services were in demand so we made a pretty good living.

Life was great. We were so happy being together twenty-four hours a day. Even though my duties as a written-test examiner had come to an end and we no longer did the ground schools, the checkrides kept Bob very busy and the paperwork, scheduling and domestic duties kept me busy. We had a nice home, good friends, comfortable lifestyle, and no major worries. Well, I guess all good things eventually come to an end, but it was not supposed to happen overnight. After twenty years of being able to overcome all the obstacles life threw in our way, I was at a total loss after Bob's heart problem flared up.

Was Bob going to be OK? Could I take proper care of him? How long would our savings last? Despite all those years with the FAA, Bob had no medical or retirement benefits since he was on contract with the federal government. What were we going to do? I became a nervous wreck. I could not eat or sleep, nor stay still. I lost forty pounds, looked tired all the time and drove poor Bob crazy. The stress I put myself under was terrible. I felt like it was up to me to take care of everything. Bob was unable to fly so he started teaching flight instructor ground schools at an international flight school and did what I would let him do around the house. I was afraid of him having a heart attack so I did all the strenuous work and the worrying for both of us, which was a big mistake. After all those months of self-imposed stress, I wore myself out and was faced with going to the hospital.

After I told Bob about the panic alert and the need to check it out at the hospital, my last words before we left the house were, "It will only take a few minutes to get a blood test. I'm sure it's all a big mistake. I feel fine." A couple hours later, we were sitting in the lab waiting room. That is an appropriate name for the little cubbyhole we were stuck in, waiting for an answer.

One of the lab techs finally appeared and said, "Mrs. Burroughs . . . good news. Your platelets are OK. You can go home now." Exhaling a big sigh of relief, I grabbed my purse and headed down the hallway towards the double doors and freedom. I wanted to get out of there before they changed their minds. Only a few more steps . . . reach for the door handle . . .

"Mrs. Burroughs, Mrs. Burroughs, wait a minute, please." I had my hand on the door but I could not go any further. I was frozen to the floor. My brain was saying, "Go, go" but I could not move. My dear wonderful hubby put his arm around my shoulder giving me the strength to turn around and face the lab tech who had now caught up with us.

"Mrs. Burroughs, I am so sorry but I looked at the wrong results at first. You need to go around to the ER. I am so sorry." I just stood there. This cannot be happening to me. My memory of getting from that spot to the ER is a little hazy. I am sure Bob took charge since I had turned into a quivering lump of Jell-O. All I remember is sitting in another waiting room and going to the bathroom every thirty minutes. The vaginal bleeding was worse than ever. It was very embarrassing to have to ask a nurse for pads, but I had no choice.

Finally, after several hours of nervously glancing through every magazine available, my name was called and we were ushered into a curtained-off cubicle. By that time, I was absolutely miserable. I had not eaten since early that morning. I was bleeding profusely and very uncomfortable. All I wanted to do was go home. More blood was drawn for testing and so many questions were being asked. My mind was not functioning properly and my answers were quite vague. The medical personnel probably thought I was totally incompetent. Finally everyone left and Bob and I were alone in that cold and very inhospitable (pardon the pun) place. Neither one of us knew what to expect, the waiting made us both extremely nervous. At last we heard voices outside our cubicle and one of the doctors walked in.

"Well," the ER doctor said, "your platelet levels are falling fast. Yesterday they were 11, this morning they were 4, and now they are 2. Something needs to be done right now."

"What does that mean? I don't know what all those numbers mean," I whimpered, "and why do I have all these bruises and the red dots all over my legs?"

The doctor explained, "Your platelets should be over 140 to be in the normal range. Without the platelets, your blood will not clot. The bruises and red dots, which are called petechiae, are the result of the low platelets. Your blood is actually leaking through the walls of your capillaries and up through the pores in your skin causing the red dots. With your platelets so low, you are in danger of hemorrhaging either internally or externally. It's a good thing you did not wait any longer before you came to the hospital."

"Oh, OK" was my tremulous answer. That was the beginning of my struggle with Immune Thrombocytopenic Purpura.

****

Yesterday I meet a set of twins, both with ITP. Just to give you an idea of how messed up this stuff is (ITP), they are on different treatment plans. Why you ask, I asked the same thing! One does IVIg with no problem; the other went into a 4-day coma. Whatever the meds or treatment, if twin "A" can do it twin "B" can't. I figured out some time ago that what works for you will not work for me. Oh yea, one went into a 2-year remission while the other was all over the place with platelet counts. I've got better odds at hitting the lottery than figuring out how to handle this. So I go with the flow!!

Hap Hapner - Miami, FL

2 FIVE DAYS AND NIGHTS IN PCU

The rollercoaster ride the platelets takes can get very exhaustive and frustrating. We just need to be positive and trust that the doctors are doing the right thing to solve the problem...

Jay Jacinto - Anaheim, CA

My first night in the hospital was miserable. A monitor was hung around my neck with wires taped to my chest; IVs were connected to both arms pumping all kinds of strange stuff into me like plasma, platelets and gamma globulin. The platelet infusion was painful and no fun. It was still partially frozen and the nurse had to use a syringe to force the icy concoction into my vein. Other medical personnel were in and out of my room, bombarding me with questions that I was too confused to answer, or drawing vials of blood. Meanwhile, I could not go to the bathroom and my pad was overflowing. I was a bloody mess. All I wanted to do was crawl under the bed and hide.

Bob had to make a quick run back home to feed the dogs and get some clean clothes for me. I was more worried about him than myself while he was gone. I was afraid the stress and strain of the situation, plus the physical exertion of dealing with our four-legged monsters, might be too much for his heart. When he came walking back into my room I was so glad to see him. Not only because of the relief in knowing he was OK, but also his physical presence gave me the strength I needed to face the rest of the night. Oh, by the way, did I mention that I was scared and confused?

Dr. Haynes (from the emergency room) came by to explain what might be wrong with me but all that information went in one ear and out the other. Sometimes when I am under a lot of stress my brain function is not too efficient. Luckily Bob was there to ask the questions that I was incapable of.

It seemed the blood tests I had in the ER indicated DIC. Dr. Haynes was very concerned about this condition because DIC is a life-threatening condition preventing a person's blood from clotting normally. It may cause excessive bleeding throughout the body and lead to shock, organ failure and death. DIC can be caused by infection, trauma or cancer. It is also associated with hemorrhagic fever and at that time outbreaks of Ebola and Rift Valley fever had been in the news.

Bob was extremely concerned about my problem being a form of hemorrhagic fever since he had spent half his life flying in Africa and other tropical countries, and had studied tropical diseases when he was a volunteer medical assistant at a bush hospital in Namibia. However, high fever, one of the prime symptoms of all tropical blood diseases, was not present.

A couple of weeks previously, I had gotten a really bad cut on my hand, which had become infected and my family doctor prescribed antibiotics. The cut was healing since I had been on the antibiotics for over a week, but could the infection have caused DIC?

Maybe I had cancer, not a pleasant thought. Both of my parents (now deceased) had spent the previous year going through chemotherapy; my father for lung cancer and my mother for colorectal cancer. The chemo was very hard on them both. Mom and Dad had to get treatments every week and the treatments made them sick, tired and unable to do the things they wanted to do.

"I cannot have cancer," I thought. "I do not have the time. I have a husband and my four-legged kids who depend on me. This kind of stuff happens to other people, not me."

Dr. Haynes was going to run another series of blood tests to either confirm or rule out DIC. The results would be ready the following morning. All we had to do was wait and worry. As I stated before, most of this information did not penetrate my thick skull at the time, but from the look on Bob's face after Dr. Haynes left and his cryptic answers to my questions about infections and cancer let me know this situation was not looking too good.

Looking back, I am really glad now I did not understand all the drama going on that evening. If I had, my mental state would have been as bad as my physical state and I do not believe I could have handled that.

As the evening wore on, the crowds diminished and I began to settle down. Conversation had turned to other topics and Bob had turned on the television. TV is a great way to escape reality and forget your troubles, at least temporarily. But we were destined to have one more visitor. Bob and I were talking when we noticed a gentleman dressed in a blue pinstriped suit, bright red flowered shirt and red shoes standing in the doorway. He walked in, sat in the chair and said, "Hello, my name is Dr. Renwick Goldberg. I am a hematologist from Coastal Cancer Center. I got a call to come by and see you." We did not know it at the time but this was the first of many encounters with this gentleman that were to come over the years ahead.

Dr. Goldberg did not stay very long, but in the few minutes he was there both Bob and I realized this was a man who knew what he was doing. In a short time, the doctor made his examination, asked a few questions and explained to us what he thought was going on. Of course, we had to wait for the results from all the tests, but Dr. Goldberg's apparent expertise gave us a confidence no one else had been able to do. Both of us were able to relax a little more knowing this gentleman was going to help us through this ordeal.

The rest of the evening was spent watching TV and talking to my nurse who kept a very close eye on me, but in a very friendly manner. She helped me to wash and change clothes and unhooked all the IVs so I could go to the bathroom, which was a real blessing.

Needless to say neither Bob nor I got any sleep that night. My nurse, Amelia, continued monitoring me every thirty minutes checking my blood pressure, temperature and IVs; looking at my arms, legs, chest, stomach, in my mouth; etc. She was checking for any evidence of internal bleeding. I already had petechiae and bruises, but she looked for any new bruises or swelling that could indicate internal hemorrhaging. Also if my gums started to bleed that could also indicate a worsening of my condition.

My daytime nurse, Rebecca took over early in the morning and my first full day continued in the same manner. I am surprised I did not run out of blood, so many vials were taken from me in the first twenty-four hours plus my vaginal bleeding had not slacked off either.

Early the first morning, Dr. Haynes came by and told us I probably did not have DIC. Since the second batch of blood work showed totally different results from the initial tests, the doctor attributed the first diagnosis to be wrong due to laboratory error. Easy for him to say, he was not up all night worrying about cancer or if I was going to live or not. The diagnosis was now another type of blood disorder called Immune or Idiopathic Thrombocytopenic Purpura (ITP).

When this disorder was first recognized and being studied, the 'I' stood for idiopathic since the origins of the disease were a mystery but now, since research has shown ITP to be related to a dysfunction of the immune system the 'I' stands for immune.

What causes ITP? In some people, certain drugs like quinine or sulfa-like drugs and even some antibiotics can lower platelet counts, or it may be associated with other diseases such as non-Hodgkin's lymphoma, or infections such as HIV or hepatitis. Helicobacter Pylori, the bacteria that cause stomach ulcers, has also been tied to the lowering of platelet counts and diagnosis of ITP. At the time of this writing there are studies being conducted around the world to determine if there are environmental or food intolerance triggers, but so far no conclusive results are available. In most people like me the cause is unknown, hence the original term idiopathic.

There are two types of ITP, acute and chronic. Acute ITP is found mainly in children and is associated with the body's reaction to a virus. This usually disappears with time and treatment. Only a small percentage of children diagnosed will develop chronic ITP. The most feared complication is intracranial hemorrhage, a bleeding in the brain, like a stroke. Fortunately, this is rare, occurring in less than one half to one percent of the children diagnosed with ITP. Chronic ITP is found mainly in adolescents and adults and is much more difficult to cure. In fact, there is no sure cure; only treatments to control the production and protection of platelets.

ITP is classified as an autoimmune disorder, meaning the body's immune system produces autoantibodies that attach to proteins on the patient's platelets, which causes them to be destroyed by the body's white blood cells, mainly in the spleen or liver. Since platelets are what cause the blood to clot and seal tiny holes in blood vessels, a low platelet count can result in blood seeping through the walls of capillaries, veins and arteries leading to external signs such as unexplained bruising, bleeding gums or noses and petechiae. ITP can also cause internal hemorrhaging in the stomach, brain, kidneys or liver.

Of course I did not learn any of this information until I was home and had access to our computer. A website that proved very helpful in our understanding autoimmune disorders is hosted by AARDA (American Autoimmune Related Diseases Association). We learned that ITP is one of over a hundred disorders caused by a malfunction of the immune system. Some other autoimmune diseases include type 1 diabetes, lupus, rheumatoid arthritis, Meniere's disease, psoriasis, Hashimoto's thyroiditis, Crohn's disease, cardiomyopathy, multiple sclerosis, and vasculitis just to name a few. According to AARDA's website, http://www.aarda.org, the term 'autoimmune disease' refers to a varied group of illnesses that involve almost every human organ system. It includes diseases of the nervous, gastrointestinal, and endocrine systems, as well as skin and other connective tissues, ears, eyes, blood and blood vessels.

In all of these diseases, the underlying problem is similar - the body's immune system becomes misdirected and attacks the very organs it was designed to protect. Instead of responding to and destroying foreign bacteria and viruses, the immune system targets healthy cells, tissues and organs and produces antibodies to attack them, resulting in a wide variety of disorders.

What causes the body's immune system to start targeting cells, tissues and organs is still unknown. Scientists are still searching to find the reason why the body should unexpectedly start producing an immune response to itself. It is known that there is a genetic link that increases a person's chances of developing an autoimmune disease; however, genetic predisposition is not the only factor. There are a number of triggers playing a part such as bacteria, viruses, toxins, hormones, significant stress, some drugs and the latest find, environmental factors.

Virginia Ladd, president and executive director of AARDA said, "Autoimmune diseases are increasing and we think the environment is playing a role since autoimmune disorders have increased so much in the last decade. We know there is a genetic factor, but genes do not change that fast. Very little research has been done concerning this link; much more research is needed."

The first autoimmune disease was discovered in the 1950s. After that, many other diseases were found to be autoimmune responses. Through this research, progress has been made finding new treatments for various disorders caused by the malfunctioning immune system resulting in a better quality of life, but what initiates the problem is still a mystery.

An article on the AARDA website states that autoimmune diseases are still not well-known or well-understood by the medical and research community and a large part of the general population of our country is still not aware that the problem even exists. Because these diseases cross the different medical specialties, such as rheumatology, endocrinology, hematology, neurology, cardiology, gastroenterology and dermatology, and because such specialties usually focus on singular diseases within their particular category, there has been little focus on autoimmunity as the underlying cause.

According to a 2001 survey by the Autoimmune Diseases Association, over 45 percent of patients with autoimmune diseases have been labeled chronic complainers in the earliest stages of their illness. Tragically, many of these patients suffer significant damage to their organs in the meantime and end up carrying this health burden with them for the rest of their lives because of the delay in diagnosis. The fact that women have enhanced immune systems compared to men increases women's resistance to many types of infection, but also makes them more susceptible to autoimmune diseases.

Ladd believes this disease category is not getting the attention it deserves. "Autoimmune disorders are an under recognized significant health issue in the United States mainly because each disease is thought of singularly, but together autoimmune disorders affect 50 million Americans and that count is growing exponentially. Autoimmune diseases are one of the top ten causes of death in women under the age of 65 and according to a report by the National Institute for Environmental Health Studies, it is number one."

Autoimmune diseases have a genetic link mainly passed on through the female line. For example, if a mother has rheumatoid arthritis, her daughter may have another type of disorder such as Crohn's disease and the granddaughter may develop another type of autoimmune disease such as ITP.

AARDA stresses that if the public, particularly women, and medical practitioners were more aware of the genetic predisposition to develop autoimmune disease, clearly there would be more emphasis on taking a medical history regarding autoimmune diseases within the family when presented by a patient with confusing symptoms. Earlier screening of these diseases could not only prevent significant and lifelong health problems but also actually prevent some autoimmune diseases. Taken together, autoimmune diseases strike women three times more than men. Some diseases have an even higher incidence in women. In fact, of the 50 million Americans living with autoimmunity, 30 million people are women, some estimates say. Moreover, these diseases represent the fourth largest cause of disability among women in the United States. (U.S. Department of Health and Human Services, Office on Women's Health. Women's Health Issues: An Overview. Fact sheet. May 2000.)

This information has been reprinted from http://www.aarda.org/women_and_autoimmunity.php. To find out more about autoimmune disorders, contact AARDA at AMERICAN AUTOIMMUNE RELATED DISEASES ASSOCIATION, 22100 Gratiot Avenue, Eastpointe, MI 48021-2227, Ph 586.776.3900 or http://www.aarda.org.

****

Gladly I did not know anything about autoimmune diseases, ITP, platelets or how close I came to bleeding to death that first night in the hospital. I was not overjoyed at my enforced confinement, but if I had known exactly how my dropping platelet count could have had such dire consequences, I would have been a basket case.

Overall, I cannot complain though. I had the same two nurses for the five days and nights I was in PCU and they were angels, treating me like a queen the whole time. Up until that time, I had had so much nervous energy since Bob's heart problems, I never stayed still. I had to be constantly moving or doing something. This enforced bed rest was tough at first, but became easier with each passing day. I have to admit to enjoying the royal treatment, being waited on hand and foot. Bob and the nurses kept me supplied with drinks, ice cream and cookies and I was very seldom left alone. Bob had to go home and take care of our four-legged kids every day but while he was gone, friends and family were either with me in person or calling me on the phone. My parents lived three hundred miles away but called two or three times a day. Mom and Dad were not in good health themselves, both of them were battling cancer but they were very concerned about Bob and me. That meant a lot to us.

It was not all fun and games though. Even though not feeling sick, I was in very serious condition. At the time, I thought the nurses checked in with me every thirty minutes because they wanted to. Later on I found out my condition was 'guarded' and the girls had to keep a very close eye on me. I was still bleeding profusely and my hemoglobin and platelets were way below the normal range. The big fear was hemorrhaging either internally or externally. That was why they examined my arms, legs and mouth and also why I had to wear a monitor.

Dr. Goldberg showed up bright and early every morning. His confidence and positive attitude were encouraging. It was either the second or the third morning he told us all the blood work confirmed ITP. He took me completely off the antibiotic I was still taking for my cut hand. It was almost totally healed by that time and there was the possibility the antibiotic was contributing to my problem.

There are no known cures for this disorder, and the treatments depend on each individual patient. The standard first step is to rule out any infections such as H. pylori or medications that could lower the platelet count. That was already accomplished and I was hooked to an IV drip of immunoglobulin, a type of antibody, also referred to as IVIg along with the plasma and was started on Prednisone. This corticosteroid is usually used as a first line treatment for ITP. It is initially administered in large doses to attack and destroy the autoantibodies that attach to the platelets. The medication is slowly tapered off as platelet counts increase.

If my platelet count did not improve with the Prednisone, the next step was a bone marrow examination. This would verify that there were adequate platelet forming cells and to rule out other diseases such as metastatic cancer and leukemia. One of the nurses told me that the bone marrow test was very painful and uncomfortable so I was not looking forward to the possibility of going through the exam.

Miraculously, the Prednisone had a positive result, therefore no need for the bone marrow test. My platelet count started to increase but my hemoglobin was still dangerously low. Being extremely anemic, Dr. Goldberg wanted to do a red blood cell transfusion. We waited for a couple of days for the transfusion but for some unknown reason the hospital could never find a match. My platelet count continued to climb and I was starting to get a little stir crazy, so the good doctors decided they were tired of dealing with me and sent me home with strict orders to rest and stay out of trouble. That, my friend, was easier said than done.

****

My low platelet condition was discovered a year and a half ago in an annual company medical (70k at the time). My numbers continued to drop for six months until I was referred to a hematologist, who determined that I have a protein clone that was attacking my platelets. My numbers were somewhat stable in the 30,000s without any drug treatments. I have had three sessions of IVIg over the past six months that 'temporarily' raised levels back over 300,000 each time, without side effects. I have none of the visible symptoms; fatigue is an issue when my numbers are low. We have not yet used any of the medications that are available. My hematologist has suggested that I would be a good candidate for a splenectomy. Before my referral, I did a lot of thinking about a specific cause of my numbers. I had a large deep bruise from a sports injury about the same time as my medical – was this a cause or a symptom? I had a large weight loss three years ago; did this trigger something? I am a chronic worrier (work, family); is ITP stress induced?

I have done a lot of youth volunteering work requiring long, late hours at certain times of year – did I burn myself out? I may never know if it is one thing or a combination of things; it sounds like many of us never will. My wife and I consider it lucky to have found this when we did and that I am being looked after before it could have been much worse or even too late. It has corrected some priorities. Social networking has been a godsend in learning how many others really have this, and how other people have been treated and how they have responded, favorably or unfavorably. We all want to get better, but we also need to let people know that this is more common than anyone knows. When I talk to other people about what we have, they know of others with our symptoms. Getting this talked about in the mass media will be the first step in finding the causes and the cures.

Dale Paynter - Cambridge, Ontario, Canada

3 HOME SWEET HOME

I've just started this journey. Still learning things and working on the best plan for me. We are all so different even while we are the same.

Dale Paynter – Cambridge, Ontario, Canada

Home at last, what a wonderful feeling to be back where I belonged. Things were going to be very different though. No more running around, staying busy all the time. Dr. Goldberg lectured me soundly on only doing only what had to be done and nothing more. Bob promised the good doctor he would make sure I followed those instructions. I did not realize at first doing nothing was harder than staying busy.

My week in the hospital was an ordeal I never want to repeat, but I did learn some very interesting things I would never have learned if this experience had not happened. I learned Bob was not as delicate as I had originally thought. He had coped with my illness, a sixty-mile round trip twice a day between the house and hospital, lack of sleep, the dogs and all the stress and strain associated with the past week. He was very tired but determined to take care of me. I also learned I had not needed to put myself through all that worry and stress during the past year, not letting him do anything strenuous for fear of him having a heart attack. I realized he was stronger than I thought. He had wanted to take more of an active role in the day-to-day chores, but did not want to hurt my feelings by saying so. At that particular point in time, knowing that Bob could handle more responsibilities was very reassuring, because now Bob had to take over and do all those tedious little jobs involved with housework and having seven dogs as well as teach his ground school classes.

Needless to say, it was not as easy for Bob as it had been for me. I had many, many years of experience and had a daily routine – get out of bed; wash and dress; get the dogs organized, pottied and fed; our breakfast; sweep, mop, vacuum, dust, laundry, etc. Easy for me, not so for my poor hubby; I had to cut him some slack though since he was still working three days a week.

What made it even harder for me, I was on 80 mg of Prednisone. I had more get up and go than before I got sick. I was so wired and HUNGRY all the time. Several people had told me how Prednisone increased appetite, but good Lord I wanted to eat, eat and eat some more. The first day I went with Bob to his ground school, I made a big mistake and did not take any food with me. My husband did not trust me to stay at home by myself. He knew I would not sit still and take it easy. Bob knew me too well.

The vending machine people made some money that day until I ran out of change. Luckily I had taken some paperwork with me, which kept my mind occupied, but by the time Bob finished his class at 5:00, I was actually faint from hunger. I could not walk unassisted; I was so shaky. All I could think about was 'Gotta eat! Gotta eat! Food! Food!' This was a new and scary experience for me. Granted, I have gone without a meal on occasion and had hunger pangs but never this overpowering feeling. I could not even wait until we got home to eat. We stopped at a local steakhouse with a buffet, and believe me I got my money's worth that night. Heck with the salads, I got every meat available. I think I went back to the buffet three or four times; then came the desserts, chocolate heaven. I had lost a lot of weight before I was diagnosed with ITP and could stand to gain a few pounds back, but eating at this rate, I would become a blimp in a few months' time.

Something had to be done. The next day I started 'grazing.' Every hour or so, I would eat a sandwich or fruit or yogurt. The craving for sweets was still overpowering and I would give in every once in a while but grazing kept me from going hog wild again.

The original problem of not being able to stay still had not been solved though. It was impossible to sit and read or watch TV, and I did not feel sick. I felt so energetic and ready to do anything. Bob got so mad at me when I started going stir-crazy and had to move around, even if I just walked back and forth in the house. I tried to explain to him I had so much energy due to the medication, but he never understood why I could not sit still.

He caught me doing some housework several times and thoroughly blessed me out. We finally compromised and he would let me do non-strenuous jobs like laundry, washing dishes, sweeping, etc., but no walking dogs or vacuuming. Sounds familiar, but the shoe was on the other foot. Now he was trying to do all the work and worrying for both of us.

Our dogs have been mentioned several times and I think some introductions are in order. First of all, we never intended to have so many dogs. It just happened. We live out in the country where irresponsible people dump their unwanted pets. For some reason, these poor creatures wandered into our yard with no prompting from us. Somehow they knew we would not hurt them even though we tried to ignore each new arrival hoping he/she would move along. Unfortunately not all of them took the hint.

Our first acquisition was Spike. He was one of three very young puppies Bob found on the side of the road. We did not do anything at first, hoping their momma would come and get them. No luck. It was the middle of winter and we could not leave them unprotected overnight so we took them home with us. We found homes for the other two but Spikey stole our hearts. What a devil he was. He tore up books, magazines, shoes, furniture, and rugs, whatever he could find to chew on. He ate a poison toad and I had to rush him to the vet. We almost lost him but the tough little guy pulled through. He grew into a very smart dog even though a little funny-looking. He had German shepherd colorings with a bulldog build. Think about it, a German shepherd with short bowed legs, quite unique.

Next came Annie. The poor girl was just a fur coat stretched over a pile of bones. She had not had a real meal in a long time. What attracted us to her was her happy smiling face with one ear sticking straight up and the other ear turned downed from the tip. Even though she had had a rough life, the little girl was full of joy and happiness. We simply had to give her something to eat and she has been with us ever since. That is how we got our 'Little Orphan Annie.'

Just a few weeks later a strange black dog showed up in the yard with a rope tied around his neck with the end trailing along behind him. We could tell he had chewed the rope free from wherever he was staked and ran away from home. Bob and I ignored him and did not feed or pet him for about a week hoping he would give up and go home. No luck. We asked everyone we knew if a big black lab puppy could come and live at his or her house; again, no luck.

The poor creature was getting pretty skinny so we broke down and fed him. The big guy had a personality just like Annie and was so full of love. He was quite accident-prone though. He did not pay attention to his surroundings when he was playing and consistently ran into the house or cars or trees. Of course we got attached to the big goof and he became our Max. We named him Max because three was the maximum number of dogs we were going to keep. Yeah right.

Max and Annie hit it off immediately. They played together constantly but unfortunately, Annie came into heat before we got either of them "fixed." Several months later we had five additions to the family.

Just imagine the two of us, three young active dogs and five newborn monsters in a little 12 by 50 foot mobile home. What a zoo! It was not too difficult to find homes for four of the puppies, but the fifth one was a problem. She was the runt of the litter and from the very beginning she was scared of everything and everybody. Whenever someone would come to look at the puppies, the other four would run around and do all the cute puppy things but she would run the other way and hide. Well guess what, we had our fourth dog, Heidi. It is easy to see how she got her name. She was always hiding. We hoped the little girl would grow out of her fear of everything and everybody but no such luck.

Heidi grew into a paranoid, neurotic, hyperactive dog driving us all crazy. We tried training and medication but she was still scared of her own shadow. Heidi ate more than all the other dogs but she stayed skinny due to her constant pacing and barking at every sound and movement. She was a pain, but she adored Bob and me. We were the only people she would come near so we were stuck with her.

That was it…. NO MORE DOGS!!!!

Spike, Annie, Max and Heidi made life very interesting especially if they all escaped into the yard at the same time. One at a time was no problem. He/she would stay within calling distance, but if two or more got out together they were gone for hours. Chain-link fence solved that problem, but we made a big mistake. We should have gotten a six-foot fence. We learned that lesson with dog number five.

One morning our four monsters were out in the fence doing what dogs normally do first thing in the morning. They always bark at whatever dogs bark at but that particular morning the barking was different. I finally gave in and went out to investigate. What I saw was a real heartbreaker. Sitting in the middle of the yard was the most pitiful looking creature I had ever seen. He looked like he was at death's doorstep; no hair, filthy, skinny, very weak and needing immediate attention. We put him in the patio and gave him a little bit to eat followed by a gentle sudsy bath. The following day we took him to the vet and found out he had every worm imaginable (except heartworm), a backside full of birdshot and both kinds of mange. It took weeks of work to get the guy back in shape but he was so friendly and happy, it was worth it. He grew into a beautiful chocolate lab named Charlie Brown.

When he was well enough to meet the other dogs we let him out in the fence with them. That was when we discovered that a four-foot fence was no match for that boy. But after a lot of training (and treats) he learned to do as he was told with only a few lapses and stayed in the fence most of the time.

Next came Baby. The cutest, sweetest bulldog with a tail that wagged so fast, her backend could not keep up and she would plop on the ground. At that point, I was so busy taking care of our six mutts, I did not have time for much else. Much of the day was spent working with the two latest arrivals, training them to stay in the yard and to come when called. I found homes for Charlie and Baby but Bob was too attached to them and would not let them go. He was only at home in the evenings and did not realize what a chore it was to keep those guys trained and clean enough to stay in the house at night.

Then the medical problems started. Bob usually spent five or six days a week doing checkrides or other flying activities until his knee started giving him problems.

A baker's cyst had developed on the back of his knee joint and got as big as a baseball and required surgery but the cyst popped before the surgery could be performed. What a mess! His orthopedic surgeon, Dr. Yates, did what he could to clean out all the infection and necrotic tissue but a couple of months later, Bob was back in the hospital for more surgery. He had developed an infected blood clot in the same spot swelling up like the original cyst and popping as well.

That time, the surgery was more extensive. A lot more necrotic tissue had to be removed leaving a hole in the back of his leg, which was five inches long, three inches wide and two inches deep. It took months for it to heal. I had to clean and pack it twice a day. Meanwhile, Bob was unable to work for six months. Luckily at that time we had a good bit of savings to live on.

After Bob recovered from that traumatic experience, he slowly started flying again. Not as much as before the surgeries, but as much as he could do with a very stiff leg. After about a year, things started to get back to normal. Bob was flying full-time and we were not too worried about his leg. It was not causing any problems and we were confident that all the infection was gone which was a mistake because it started swelling again. Luckily we caught it in time and a course of strong antibiotics took care of the problem.

Needless to say the entire daily dog training went out the window during that time and Charlie and Baby reverted to their bad habits, but my first priority was my husband. We coped with the dogs as best we could. Baby was restricted to staying inside the fence and Charlie spent most of his time in the house, walking him on the leash whenever he needed to go out.

I never got back in the training regimen since I was going to the airport with Bob whenever he went flying. He wanted me to be with him just in case something happened. One day on our way back home, we spied what we thought was a familiar head poking out of the weeds along the side of our dirt road. "Oh no, Charlie escaped again," was our first reaction but as we looked closer we realized it was an unfamiliar face so we continued on towards our house. The next thing we knew, there was a dog running as fast as he could, following us down the road. We lost sight of him before we turned into our yard so we figured he had given up on catching us. Wrong...about a half-hour later, our monsters informed us that we had company. In the yard sat a very tired panting black and white puppy that seemed very proud of himself for accomplishing his task of tracking us down.

I was totally against having any more dogs and refused to have anything to do with him, but as usual he would not leave. I put up fliers trying to find another home for him but before anyone could call he was hit by a truck speeding down our road and very badly injured. Twelve hundred dollars later we had another dog, Tippy, named for the white tips on his toes and tail.

All seven dogs got along great at first but trouble began when Tippy and Charlie started fighting. It got so bad that we had to keep them separated twenty-four hours a day. When Tippy and Max started fighting, we had to keep them separated, then Max and Charlie started fighting, then Baby and Heidi as well. It turned out that we had to keep Charlie and Heidi in one room, Max and Baby in another room, Tippy in the bathroom, and Annie and Spike wherever they fitted in.

All this tension and fighting between the kids started after Bob developed his heart problems. Bob and I were both very scared and stressed at that time and the emotional distress transmitted to the dogs. A new pen in the back yard for Tippy, Annie and Baby solved some of the problems, but we still had to keep Charlie and Max separated during the day and everybody sorted between different rooms in the house at night.

Between the dog circuses, worrying about Bob, trying to do all the work and worrying about finances, no wonder I got sick and wound up in the hospital. I still do not know how Bob dealt with it all while I was not there to help. When I got back home from the hospital neither one of us was able to do the running around that was necessary to keep the peace between our four-legged children, something had to be done.

A solution to the dog problem came in the person of our dear friend, Silke. She took Charlie home with her even though she had enough of a handful with a full-time job, a young daughter and another puppy and kitten already demanding all her attention. That was the type of person she was and still is, always ready to help even if it was more than she could handle. I was very leery of this arrangement because I knew Charlie could be a royal pain if he escaped the confines of the yard. That did happen but patient Silke never gave up. She found another loving home for the big goofy dog and he is still there today.

My suggestion of finding another home for Tippy, who had instigated all the fighting to begin with, was overruled by my better half so we came up with another solution. With Charlie gone, we put Max and Heidi in the back pen and the other four all got along great so there was no problem keeping them in the house. Problem solved, except I was not happy with two of my children being left outside all day and having to spend the night in the barn. They were not getting the love and attention they deserved but at the time, there was nothing else we could do.

Max and Heidi did not complain and seemed to enjoy their fate. We made up for some of the lost time every night when I took them for a walk and put them to bed in the barn. I would talk and play with my two kids while feeding them. Before I left every evening, Max would put his front legs around my neck and hug me.

We may have had serious medical conditions keeping us from doing things we wanted or needed to do, but we had a special something keeping us going; the undying love of our four-legged kids. Nothing, not heart problems nor ITP was ever going to change that.

****

We found out my two and a half-year-old little girl had ITP in March. Saw bruising but passed it off cause she's so active and hyper; then came the bloody nose. We took her in and she was at 6,000. Her head bruises were pretty bad so we had to go the next day to Stanford where she had already dropped to 4,000 over night. Had her treated with IVIg. She was hooked up to the IV for 6 hours. The treatment was just a band aide though and only lasted for four weeks. She had terrible side effects of headache and vomiting. Her platelets went up for a little bit but slowly went back down to 17,000 as soon as treatment wore off. All I ever heard from her doctor's was to keep her safe. Really??? I try so hard but unless they can provide me a plastic bubble there is no way to keep this little girl down! She doesn't know she's sick. Stress is a major factor in platelet destruction... so I've read and I heard it's autoimmune? So I have backed off on potty training (cause it seems to stress her out) and taking her pacifier away. I have also taken steps to treating her in the "autoimmune sense" which has a lot to do with diet and allergies. She no longer gets dairy (highly inflammatory), only soy and vegan milk and cheeses. We are trying to go all organic, a lot less sugar, and I'm giving her raw locally farmed honey. The doctors can't tell us much because there's so little they know, so it's up to us I guess? I haven't had to do any treatments anymore and frankly don't want to cause it's hard on her little body. Her platelets are now maintaining on their own and haven't dropped below 30,000 and are as high sometimes as 140,000. My doctors try to say the diet has nothing to do with it but seriously how can they say for sure when they don't even know about this disease themselves? This is so hard and frustrating, scary, and overwhelming! I cry almost every day. I'm scared for my daughter and stressed so hard when I see her fall.

Brandy DeWitt - Hollister, CA

4 RELAPSE

It's the wonderful world of ITP........not fun. I believe that your own inner happiness has a lot to do with healing!

Jessica Wolcson McNally - Long Island, NY

Bob's ground school classes ended a few weeks after I got out of the hospital and so did the income it brought in. We were in a financial bind since neither one of us could go out and get a job due to our medical problems. The stress and strain from the past month had caught up with Bob. He was having angina pain and palpitations and, of course, I was confined to the house.

I should have still been a nervous wreck, worrying about everything but I was not. I had found a way to relax and have an inner peace that was truly amazing. We had been practicing Reiki for a few years prior to all this, but with all my 'spare time' I could now concentrate on my self healings and what a wonderful difference it made.

There is nothing magical or mystical about Reiki (pronounced as two words Rei-Ki). Basically all it involves is concentrating on the body's ability to heal itself. The name Reiki in Japanese means "universal life force". It is an ancient healing method manipulating energy flows in the body allowing the body's own natural healing ability to work. Reiki was brought to Japan in 1848 from Tibet by Dr. Usui Sensei and is similar to the ancient healing art practiced by the Old Kingdom Egyptians over four thousand years ago. Many other civilizations throughout history have used this kind of healing in one form or another. It is used to decrease pain, ease muscle tension and speed healing. Reiki is intended to be used in addition to conventional medical treatment to help reduce stress and anxiety and help with the healing process. My Reiki healings helped me to relax and gave my body the extra energy it needed to heal physically, mentally, emotionally and psychologically.

In Reiki, there are seven main energy centers in the human body similar to acupuncture or acupressure points called chakras. Energy flows through the chakras and into the body, cleansing and speeding up the healing process. My method of practicing Reiki was in the form of a prayer. I would ask God to help direct the flow of energy, then just relax and let the warmth spread from my head down to my toes. I also used visualization while doing my self-healings, directing the Reiki to zap out the antibodies that were causing the problem while protecting my platelets with an energy shield to keep any of the bad antibodies from attaching to them.

I do not know if it worked but it certainly did make me feel good, more relaxed with a really positive attitude. I felt so focused and free from stress and was genuinely happy. I am a firm believer that a person's attitude determines that person's wellness. In other words, if you have a positive attitude and believe you will succeed, you will. A negative attitude puts a damper on success whether it be battling an illness or in life itself.

Even with my newfound inner peace, I have got to admit that I was apprehensive about going to Dr. Goldberg's office for my first appointment. Bob and I had no idea what to expect. The thought of going to the 'Cancer Center' did not fill our hearts with joy. My parents were both cancer patients and I did not want to go through the sickness and lethargy they suffered after their weekly chemo treatments. Everything was a big question mark. Would I have to have chemotherapy? Am I going to be able to live a normal life? Would I get better?

Upon arrival I realized the apprehension prior to my visit was unnecessary. My platelet count had made a big jump from 13,000 to 20,000 since I had left the hospital thanks to the Reiki and 80 mg of Prednisone. The good doctor was very pleased with my improvement. My hemoglobin was still very low, but Dr. Goldberg did not seem overly concerned about that. He put me on iron supplements and if the pills did not do the trick, we would try something else. Best of all, no one mentioned anything about chemotherapy, radiation or any of those other dreadful but necessary treatments a person associates with a cancer center. Of course, I did not bring the subject up either, best not to press my luck.

Just like in the hospital, everyone I dealt with at the cancer center was so nice. I did not feel like I was in an assembly line, waiting to be processed and kicked out the door when finished. All the staff was genuinely interested in me and how I felt, not rushing through any of the procedures and actually carried on a one on one conversation with each individual patient. This was totally different from some of the busy clinics I have had experience with, not all but some. On each successive visit, Bob and I were greeted by name and treated with the same courtesy. That made life with ITP a whole lot easier.

When we got back in the examination room with Dr. Goldberg and his nurse, Angie, we had the same relaxed atmosphere. Bob and I were still not too knowledgeable about ITP and had a number of questions. All of which were answered and our course of action fully explained even though other patients were waiting. We really appreciated the care and attention. We knew we were in good hands.

At home, in our ever-continuing research on ITP over the Internet, we found a website hosted by the Scripps Institute (http://www.scripps.edu/itp). We read ITP patients may have no symptoms and the low platelet count may only be noted during routine blood studies. However, most patients see their doctor because they develop a skin rash on their legs (called petechiae, a collection of small pinpoint bruises), excessive bruising or, less commonly, bleeding from the nose, gums or rarely from the gastrointestinal tract (stomach or bowel) or genitourinary tract (blood in the urine).

The fact that women may note prolonged or heavy menstrual bleeding explained my problem and I learned symptoms may be exaggerated by certain medications, which interfere with platelet function such as aspirin or ibuprofen. Over the years, I had been taking a lot of ibuprofens for my ever present migraines.

The Scripps site also noted that with ITP, blood count is normal except for a low platelet count. Occasionally, patients are anemic if significant bleeding has occurred. Bone marrow examination is normal except that the number of megakaryocytes (the cells which produce platelets) are often increased since the body is attempting to respond to the destruction of platelets by increasing their production. Autoantibodies against platelets can be detected in most patients. In chronic ITP, all other laboratory tests should be normal, including tests to rule out HIV, hepatitis or cytomegalovirus infection.

(This information was reprinted from the Scripps website, http://www.scripps.edu/mem/itp/describe.html.)

****

According to Dr. Goldberg, there is really no rhyme or reason as to how or why people develop autoimmune disorders. He said, "The most active time is after seasonal changes, with viral infections setting off autoimmune disorders. If there is a common link, this is it." He added that stress; environmental factors and bacterial infections could also affect the immune system and bring on autoimmune disorders or cause worsening in patients.

Dr. Goldberg went on to state, "If someone with ITP gets an infection, the ITP will get worse for a short time then will improve as the infection clears up. Our bodies are designed to slow down the manufacturing of platelets while it is fighting off infections, but the natural platelet production picks back up when the invading virus is no longer a problem."

Many people with ITP have the idea that it is necessary to have a high platelet count, but that is not so. It is according to the individual's age, activity level, bleeding history, and other factors. Some ITP patients live very comfortably with a platelet count of 20,000, while other more physically active patients need to maintain a higher level.

"The issue that needs to be paid attention to with ITP is maintaining a steady platelet count and not paying so much attention to the numbers," emphasized Dr. Goldberg. "Many people can live for years with a low platelet count and have no problems, everybody's different. We need to work on an individual basis and decide what is best for each individual patient."

According to the Scripps Institute website, research has confirmed that there are no cures for any type of autoimmune disorder, but treatments are available to control the various problems associated with the diseases. Corticosteroids are the first course of action in treating patients with ITP. Prednisone is the most convenient and least expensive corticosteroid but high doses over an extended period of time can cause bad side effects. Patients are usually started with 50 to 100 mg and then tapered off the medication to lower dosages as his/her platelet count increases. The goal is to maintain a safe platelet count on doses, which do not cause significant side effects; 10 mg, or less a day.

An alternate treatment method for giving corticosteroids uses very high doses of Dexamethasone (Decadron) given in one of two ways: (1) 40 mg per day for four consecutive days, given every 28 days for six courses or (2) 40 mg per day for four consecutive days, given every 14 days for four courses.

If Prednisone or Dexamethasone do not produce the desired results, then IVIg or Immunoglobulin IV can be administered but it is very expensive and takes one or two days to complete the treatment. Anti-D (Winrho SDF) is a less expensive form of IVIg but can only be used in Rh positive patients who still have a spleen. One of the side effects of Winrho is the possible destruction of red blood corpuscles.

The effectiveness of these treatments varies from person to person. Dr. Goldberg commented, "About eighty percent of ITP patients will go into remission with first line treatments but about thirty percent of them will subsequently relapse so it is a fifty/fifty shot that they will remain in remission."

If first line treatments do not result in maintaining a safe platelet count then a splenectomy is recommended. The reason being, platelets usually circulate in the bloodstream for eight to ten days. With chronic ITP, platelet life is decreased due to the immune system targeting them for destruction. The antibodies that attach to the platelets are produced mainly in the spleen or in the bone marrow. The spleen is also rich in white blood cells, which destroy the targeted platelets. About a third of the circulating platelets are in the spleen at one time so that is where the largest part of the damage is done.

That is why the people who do not respond to the corticosteroids are advised to get a splenectomy. If a splenectomy is not successful in stopping the low platelet problem, the antibodies are being produced in the bone marrow and the white blood cells are busy doing their destructive work in the bone marrow or the liver. Removal of the spleen supposedly gives the highest cure rate of all treatments but it does not work for everyone. Some ITP patients have accessory spleens and the surgeon has to remove all splenic material or the spleen can grow back.

Surgery can be done the old fashioned way, through a standard incision in the abdomen or with laparoscopy, where several small incisions are made in the abdomen and a telescope-like instrument (laparoscope) is inserted. After the blood vessels are tied, the spleen is encased in a bag and ground up so that it can be removed through the small opening. Laparoscopic surgery is associated with less post-operative side effects, a shorter recovery period and results are as good as those obtained with standard surgery. http://www.scripps.edu/mem/itp/firstrx.html)

****

Some ITP patients elect to take a wait-and-see approach and decide against having a splenectomy. Instead they elect to try second-and-third-line treatments. There are lots of options to choose from but all treatments have potential side effects and every person is unique as to what works and what does not.

Rituxan or Rituximab has brought about remission in many people. Rituxan reduces the number of B cells in your body. B cells are a type of white blood cells that, when activated, multiply and produce antibodies. Since

Rituxan reduces the number of B cells that contain CD20, it reduces the total number of cells that produce antibodies. This may include the antibodies that attach to platelets. There is also evidence that Rituxan alters T cells, another type of white blood cell, and that this may be the reason that Rituxan raises the platelet count of some patients with ITP.

The short-term response rate for Rituxan is about 60 percent. About 40 percent of patients achieve a longer-term rise in platelet count. The IV drug is generally administered once a week over a four-week period. Allergic reactions such as difficulty breathing, restricted or sore throat can occur if the Rituxan drip is too fast. Usually that is remedied with Benadryl and slowing the drip down.

Immunosuppressants (Azathioprine, Cyclosporine and Mycophenolate Mofeti) are sometimes used when the more common treatments for ITP fail to raise the platelet count. These drugs were designed for use in organ transplant patients to decrease the body's tendency to reject the new transplants. Because they deactivate the immune system, they have been used to treat a number of autoimmune diseases.

Danazol, a modified testosterone is an older treatment that is not used very much anymore. It is a synthetic androgen (male sex hormone) that disrupts the production of estrogen. Danazol is considered a second-line treatment for ITP, used after other treatments are considered or fail. It does not have the side effects of corticosteroids and can benefit some patients who cannot tolerate any of the other treatments.

ITP was once thought to be only a disease of platelet destruction, but recent research has shown that many people with ITP also have a platelet production problem. The newest treatment approach for treating ITP is the use of platelet growth factors such as Nplate (injection) and Promacta (pills). These agents increase platelets by stimulating the bone marrow to produce more platelets.

The use of platelet growth hormones has had mixed results. Sometimes platelets are quickly increased and other times; there is very little response. The most common adverse reactions are joint and muscle pain, dizziness, insomnia, indigestion, and a 'pins and needles' sensation. There is a potential for patients to develop reticulum (fibrous growths) in the bone marrow and also for the platelet count to drop below the pre-treatment count if the treatment is discontinued.

As a third-line treatment, Vincristine or Cyclophosphomide, which are chemotherapy agents, can be used. Chemotherapy agents can reduce the number of white blood cells and increase the chance of getting an infection. The most frequently reported side effects of Vincristine are peripheral neuropathy (reduced sensation in fingers and toes), electrolyte imbalance, constipation, and hair loss.

Cyclophosphomide side effects include chemotherapy-induced nausea and vomiting, stomachache, diarrhea, and infertility. Delayed effects include the risk of developing bladder cancer or other tumors. This is only a short description of second and third-line treatments from the Platelet Disorder Support Association's (PDSA) website. For more details, go to http://www.pdsa.org/treatments.html.

****

Even though ITP is a chronic blood disorder, some people have a spontaneous remission after six months or so on corticosteroids, where platelet levels stabilize and no further measures such as other treatments or splenectomy are needed. Up until that point, we were hoping that would be our luck. Unfortunately, wishes do not always come true.

Throughout May and June and into July everything went great. I was worried about having my periods, but they were normal with no excessive bleeding. My platelet count kept rising even though the Prednisone was decreased from 80 mg to 60, 40, 20, 10, then even down to 10 mg every other day. Everything was looking great. I still had my positive outlook. Bob was no longer stressed and having angina pain and he had even started doing some flight instruction.

We were still in a financial pickle but things were looking up and we started planning for the future. Bob had published a novel a couple of years earlier, (*Riders of the Wind* by Robert F. DeBurgh) and started working on his second book again. The writing had been put on hold due to all our medical problems. But now he was more relaxed and could concentrate on his writing. Bob has a wonderful talent for writing. *Riders of the Wind* was very successful and many readers were bugging him to finish the second novel in the series, *Winds of Fate*.

I started writing as well. I spent a lot of years as a preschool and elementary school teacher before we were married, so I put that experience to the test and wrote a series of children's picture books called *Patchwork Dog and Calico Cat*. I also started this narrative as an ongoing project until I had this ITP thing whipped.

We were so happy and the future looked so bright. Then disaster struck.

My platelet count had been going up every time I visited Dr. Goldberg even with the reduced doses of medication. The doctor had gradually lowered my dose of Prednisone to 10 mg every other day. About a week after I started the lower dose of medicine, I noticed some changes. My energy level decreased and I started getting very accident prone, running into things, bruising and twisting my ankle. My happy positive attitude started going down the drain and by my next appointment at the Cancer Center, I felt terrible. I had no energy and bruises covered my legs and arms. I kept saying to myself, "I am not going back to the hospital, NO, NO."

On July 27, when I got my CBC at the Cancer Center, all our dreams of living happily ever after came to an abrupt end. My platelets had plummeted from 92,000 down to 28,000 over a period of two weeks and we were back where we started from three months before. What a heartbreaking disappointment not only for me and Bob, but also for Dr. Goldberg, Angie and the rest of the staff at the Cancer Center. I was afraid of having a total relapse and winding up back in the hospital, but Dr. Goldberg had another alternative. He increased my Prednisone to 40 mg and arranged for me to have an IVIg at the Cancer Center the following week.

I had the Immunoglobulin IV while I was in the hospital so I knew what to expect. It was going to take about six hours per day for two days to get the procedure accomplished but we were willing to go through that. At that point, I would have done anything to avoid going back into the hospital.

Unfortunately that was not all though. Angie set up an appointment with a local surgeon, Dr. Epstein for consultation concerning spleen surgery. Dr. Goldberg had told us several times over the past couple of months that something like this could happen. It was not unusual for a relapse to occur and if it did, a splenectomy was the next step. So we were prepared for this even though we never thought it would be necessary. We thought my ITP was under control since I had improved so much over the past few months. OK, if I have to, I have to. If the surgery takes care of the ITP, it is worth another trip to the hospital. I am not looking forward to it, but I do not have much choice.

We left Dr. Goldberg's office with a lot to think about over the next few days. But the bad news did not end there. That night I started my period. I was up every two hours changing my pad. The flow was so heavy and the cramps so bad, I could not wait until morning when I could call someone and get some help. Bob was scheduled to fly with one of his students the following day so I took a bunch of pads with me to the airport because I knew most of the day would be spent in the bathroom.

Thank goodness for cell phones. I called the Cancer Center to ask for advice and they told me to call my ob/gyn, which I did. I had been on Provera when I had the bleeding problems before but had stopped since my periods were normal in May and June. Now I was to start 20 mg Provera and continue that dosage until I saw my ob/gyn the following week. What a nightmare. I still had the weekend to go before I could see any of the doctors. The IVIg was set up for Monday and Tuesday so if I could make it through the weekend….

Monday dawned bright and beautiful and we had survived the weekend so the two of us were ready to spend all day at the Cancer Center. The Provera had slowed the bleeding to a manageable flow so I was more comfortable and ready to spend all day hooked up to the IV. Upon arrival, we were ushered into an office to speak with one of the financial advisors. We were on a payment plan already, since we were broke and could not afford my medical treatment any other way, so I was expecting her to tell us that we were going to have to make larger monthly payments or something like that. As our luck had been going lately, we got more bad news we were not expecting. The IVIg treatments were going to cost $66,000. Ouch, forget that.

Dr. Goldberg was not there so we talked to another doctor who suggested another type of IV treatment, Rituxan, which is usually used for non-Hodgkin's lymphoma patients. Also if I needed, I could still get the IVIg at the hospital for about a quarter of the price quoted to us earlier. So we went home to consider the options and wait to talk with Dr. Goldberg.

It was about ten days later when we met with our doctor. By then my period had stopped and my bumps and bruises were on the mend. My platelets were up to 53,000 but that was due to the Prednisone. The higher dosages of Prednisone keep the ITP under control but we could not depend on that long-term; the side effects were too severe. Dr. Goldberg wanted me to have the splenectomy ASAP, but our twentieth anniversary was only a few weeks away and we had already bought tickets for a show. The good doctor was not too pleased but he agreed to let us wait until after our anniversary. Anyway, the anesthesiologist we had spoken with concerning the surgery said my platelets had to be above 90,000 before he would administer any anesthesia, so Dr. Goldberg had to go along with our wishes.

That also gave us time to figure out how to pay for all this. That worried me more than the surgery. The hospital was no problem since we were already on a monthly payment program from the initial hospitalization in April. I also had payment plans with the various labs that are associated with the hospital as well. Now all we had to do was work out arrangements with the anesthesiologist and most importantly the surgeon.

We chose Dr. Aaron Epstein to do my surgery since he had assisted on Bob's knee surgery a few years earlier. He was a top-notch surgeon and also a top-notch person. Our nickname for him was 'Mr. Enthusiasm.' He always had a smile, friendly manner and a positive confident attitude that really impressed us. Also when we told him about our financial situation, he gave us his 'wholesale rate' with low monthly payments.

The surgery was scheduled for September 9, 2005. We arrived at the hospital bright and early and ready to get the surgery over with. I should have been nervous but for some reason, I was cool, calm and collected. The time I spent in pre-op went pretty quickly since I was occupied with preparing for the surgery and being briefed by various people about what was about to happen. The last person to come in my little cubbyhole was the anesthesiologist who started something flowing in my IV to help me relax. That was the last thing I remember happening until I woke up screaming from pain while the nurses were moving me from the gurney onto the bed in my hospital room. I think I scared them and am glad they did not drop me. The incision in my abdomen was stretched during the move and caused a great deal of agony. It was a rather rude awakening.

My memory of the rest of that day is quite fuzzy except for being so thirsty. I was not allowed to eat or drink prior to the operation or for the rest of the day. I was used to drinking about a gallon of tea every day so that was the worst part of the whole ordeal. No matter how nicely I asked or begged, nobody would give me anything to drink. That, my friend, was the ultimate torture. Even Bob was in on the conspiracy. He sat patiently in my room all day and was the first sight I beheld each time I aroused from sleep, but he ignored my pleas for water just like everyone else.

Other than that, there were no problems. Dr. Epstein came by to check up on me and informed me he had removed two spleens, which was a bit of a surprise. It has been known for ITP patients to have an accessory spleen but it was not too common. I had a five-inch incision down my mid-section that was quite uncomfortable and hurt like the dickens when I tried to move, but such was to be expected.

I was hoping to have laparoscopic surgery but Dr. Epstein recommended the conventional type, since he would have more room to work inside of me making sure he could find and remove all the splenic material, plus the procedure would not take as long. He did not want me to be under anesthesia for any longer than necessary. Doctor knows best, right?

My platelet count the morning after surgery was way down to 9,000, which was a big disappointment, but there were no complications, no fever, and no sign of infection. Later on during the day, I had more blood work done and the platelet count was higher so the doctor attributed the first results as 'lab error'. The nurses had me up and walking around, which was a real chore, but I got rewarded with a glass of water. Heaven in a glass, forget food, give me more water.

Dr. Epstein was pleased with my recovery thus far and told me I could go home the following day barring any problems. That thought helped me to bear the pain and look forward to the next morning. We were expecting to have several days of hospitalization but the risk of infection was too great due to my suppressed immune system. It is strange to say but I was safer at home than at the hospital, less germs floating around. But Dr. Epstein gave us a long list of do's and don'ts, mostly don'ts to abide by. He really did not have to worry; it hurt too much to move. All I wanted to do was get in my nice comfortable bed and have Bob wait on me. Little did I know what was to come next.

****

My name is Caroline. I live in CT. My ITP has been long-term (30 years) but in those 30 years, I've had far less issues than most people. I guess I would be considered to have a mild case, and I'm happy to. I found out I had ITP when I arrived at the hospital in labor on Sept. 14, 1980. Since I was scheduled for a c-section (although this was not my scheduled date), blood was drawn. The OB GYN who happened to be on that Sunday was the high-risk doctor in the practice. His first thought was that the hospital lab had made a mistake with the count so tests were done again and again, each time lower than the previous ones. I got platelets through the Red Cross and proceeded to have my oldest son who arrived safely. I continued to have a low count but didn't need treatment. I went on to have 2 more sons in 1984 and 1986 without a problem, having a course of Prednisone, basically the only treatment then (besides splenectomy), at the end of each pregnancy (even though son #3 arrived 4 weeks early). My counts for the next 18 years were done yearly at my OB GYN annual visits and averaged in the 70-80,000 range. I never had a treatment, I kept my spleen. In 2004, on my 50th birthday, I discovered I had a target rash on my back and headed to my regular doctor for a Lyme Disease test, which was negative but my platelets were quite low so she sent me to a hematologist she had consulted with. By the time I saw him, maybe a week later, my count was back to where it usually is. I continued to see the hematologist regularly, no problems. I managed, between 2003 and 2007, to have 3 knee arthroscopies, no treatment needed beforehand. In 2008, I had one more arthroscopy and my right knee partially replaced. Still no treatments! In 2010, I had my left knee totally replaced, still no treatment. In March, 2011, I arrived at the hospital to have my partial knee replacement switched to a total knee and my count was lower than expected, so the choice of anesthesia was changed from spinal to general and I received platelets during the surgery. The following day my count was lower (in the 40s from the 69 it had been on surgery day, which was lower than the 104,000 it was a week before for my pre-op) so my hematologist was consulted. He put me on a short course of Prednisone which brought up the count. 12 days later, I was completely off of it. My counts were higher for a couple of months, but now they're back to the 80,000 range where they usually are. That course of Prednisone was the 1st treatment I had since 1986, and that one had only been done because I was pregnant. So I still have ITP. It's there. It affects my other medical choices, like choices of medicines. Having bad arthritis is not something easy when you have ITP, but I've managed. My hematologist allows me an Nsaid, as it's a quality of life issue for me. In general, my arthritis has affected me a lot more than my ITP, although the ITP is much more medically complicated and difficult.

Caroline Hall - Danbury, CT

5 RELAPSE AGAIN AND AGAIN

I don't doubt that being healthy and sickness free is the best thing to ask for in life...but owning up to an illness that has no real cause or cure, and living through it makes you appreciate and enjoy the little things in your life that make you happy.

Jay Jacinto - Anaheim, CA

Home sweet home...again. For a person who had never been seriously sick before, I had made up for it in the past six months. This time around Bob had no problem making me be still for the first several weeks after my surgery. My abdominal muscles were so sore I did not want to get out of bed, much less do any work.

I felt so sorry for my husband. Everything was left up to him to do, and this time I could not help even if I wanted to. Usually most people recover in about a month from surgery, but since I had been on the Prednisone, my healing took a lot longer. Dr. Epstein laid down the law, no lifting, no bending, and no stretching. He did not want to have to open me back up and fix anything I messed up and most importantly, he did not want me to get a hernia. I followed his instructions to the letter because I did not want to go through that experience again. After several follow up visits at his office, Dr Epstein told me he never wanted to see me again and dismissed me; so far, so good.

According to the Scripps website, a splenectomy gives the highest cure rate of all treatments so we were optimistic and very pleased that the splenectomy had the desired effect on my platelet count. I had to go to the Cancer Center and get a CBC the day after I got home from the hospital. That was tough, I was so sore but the platelet count of 88,000 and three days later of 142,000 made the pain bearable...almost. During the ensuing weeks, my platelets continued to climb and Dr. Goldberg decreased my Prednisone until it was 10 mg every other day. We were nervous because the last relapse occurred at that dosage.

We kept our fingers crossed as I had another period, but it was normal and my platelets maintained around 150,000. About a month after the surgery, Dr. Goldberg took me off my medication completely. Slowly, very slowly my body allowed me to start doing things again. We felt optimistic that there were going to be no more problems.

Two weeks later, my platelets were down to 78,000. Oh no, not again. The splenectomy was supposed to control the ITP. Either the antibodies were being produced somewhere else in my lymphatic system or in my bone marrow or there was some splenic material left behind. Dr. Goldberg was not too surprised with the drop but stated that if my platelets dropped below 50,000, then I would have to go back on the Prednisone. Guess what, the following week the platelet count was 41,000 and Dr. Goldberg put me on 10 mg of Prednisone. It had only been a month and a half since my surgery so it seemed that the splenectomy had been a waste of time and money, but if I had not had the operation things could have been worse, right?

Well, it got worse. I started my period and thought it was going to be normal but after a week, it turned into a gusher. After consulting with my doctors, I went up to 20 mg on both the Prednisone and Provera to get the bleeding under control. The flow was worse than ever with big clots filling the sanitary napkins. I had to wash up and change pads every two to three hours day and night. The platelets continued to drop down to 21,000 and the bleeding did not slack off as it did before, so we upped the Prednisone to 40 mg. This relapse was worse than the first one and we were scared to death.

It took about a month for the bleeding to finally slow down and stop. My platelet count started to climb so Dr. Goldberg lowered my medication back to 30 mg. He also explained to Bob and me that we have got to stop playing the numbers game. It did not matter whether my platelets were in the 30s or the 90s, what we wanted was to have them stabilize, with no more big drops on the lowest dose of Prednisone possible. The only way to do that was to stop the bleeding. What were we supposed to do now, hysterectomy? More surgery was not feasible at that time. What other options did we have?

Our bad luck continued. When I tried to reach my ob/gyn, she was nowhere to be found. She had left her practice and disappeared, no one knew where. Her replacement was a total dimwit who knew nothing about ITP and seemed totally lost when I tried to explain the situation to him, so now we had to find another ob/gyn. Would this ever end? I consulted with our family doctor and she recommended I visit a colleague of hers but when I called for an appointment, the fee was more than we could afford at the time. I applied for Medicaid to help with all my medical expenses until we could get back on our feet financially. Any other doctors were going to have to wait until then.

Meanwhile Dr. Goldberg explained to us that my condition was now classified as refractory ITP which meant my ITP was not responding to the standard treatments (Prednisone and splenectomy) and we needed to progress to more aggressive treatments. He wanted me to do the Rituxan IV treatments.

Rituxan is most commonly used by patients with non-Hodgkin's lymphoma. This drug targets the white blood cells that had been destroying my platelets. It would be a four-to-six hour IV, once a week for four weeks. We began the Rituxan treatments on November 25 and started seeing results right away. I had some problems during the first round with my throat closing up and becoming very sore, even with the Benadryl and Tylenol they gave me, but we continued to do the other three sessions at a slower drip rate and had no more problems. As my platelet count increased, my dosages of Prednisone decreased. By the end of December, my platelets were up to 90,000 to 100,000, and I was back on 10 mg of medication every other day.

Bob and I did not know what to expect now. Every time I went down to the low dose of Prednisone something bad happened. We just held our breath and waited to see if the Rituxan continued working. Dr. Goldberg told us that the Rituxan could work as long as six months. We hoped so because on January 9, I started my period again. It seemed like it was going to stop after a week's time but again I was wrong.

December and January had been a very stressful time for us. As I stated before, both of my parents had been diagnosed with cancer and had been on chemo. My mother's cancer was under control, but she was suffering from other problems. Ever since I can remember, she has had both rheumatoid and osteoarthritis. Over the years, she has been to numerous doctors and specialists but to no avail, and now the arthritis combined with osteoporosis has severely limited her ability to get around on her own. Her back, legs and hips were very weak and walking was extremely difficult. She had to use either a walker or wheelchair to get around.

My father did all he could to take care of her and the house, but his health was not too good either. He had part of one lung removed several years earlier and recovered just fine, but his lung cancer had returned and all the chemo and radiation treatments he underwent the second time around did not work as we had hoped. The new spots on his infected lung did not grow but they did not go away either. He also had emphysema in his good lung, which resulted in him being on supplemental oxygen all the time. Added to that, in December blood clots were found in his lung and leg. He was hospitalized and administered a blood thinner to dissolve the blood clots and things started to go downhill from there.

Dad was home from the hospital for a few days, but developed breathing problems and was admitted back into the hospital with pneumonia. He had been given too much blood thinner, which caused him to start bleeding internally. Between the bleeding, pneumonia and emphysema, it was just too much for his body to take and he passed away. This was very hard on us because with all the medical issues we had had to cope with since Bob was originally in the hospital with his heart problems; my husband and I were not able to spend as much time with my parents as we wanted to. They lived three hundred miles away and the long drive to their house and back to ours in one day was too hard on Bob. We were unable to stay overnight except occasionally since our dogs would be left at home alone.

Bob and I had been up to see Dad before he died and we drove up there again to attend the funeral. I had been bleeding for about a week prior to that and did not think it was going to give me any problems while we were away from home, but as usual I was wrong. The morning of the funeral the blood flow increased dramatically. The pads that I was using could not handle the flow and within less than an hour the blood was running down my legs, drenching my clothes and leaving a trail of red everywhere I went. We were three hundred and fifty miles away from my doctors and we did not know what to do. It was very important for us to be with Mom, we did not want to desert her but we had no choice. I could not attend the funeral bleeding like I was.

We called the Cancer Center and left desperate messages on their voice mail. Needless to say we were all very upset and the emotional strain was not helping my bleeding problems. The only solution we could come up with was to get home ASAP and try to get to the Cancer Center before they closed at 5 o'clock that Friday afternoon.

The return home was all interstate highways and Bob had plenty of experience driving fast yet safely from his racing days. We covered the three hundred and fifty miles in a little over four hours only stopping for bathroom runs, but as our luck was going, the lab at the Cancer Center closed early that day. One small consolation, the bleeding was still very heavy but not like it was at Mom's house. If it had continued to pour like it had that morning, we would have had no choice but to go the emergency room at the hospital.

The following day, Saturday, our dear friend and family physician, Deborah Hipp, answered our pleas for help and squeezed me in between her other appointments. I had not found an ob/gyn yet, so Debbie approved increasing the Provera to 20 mg and did a CBC to check my platelets, which had plummeted down to 39,000.

Why me Lord, my third relapse, and the worst one yet. The emotional stress was just too much. Something had to be done, the sooner the better. Dr. Goldberg increased my Prednisone to 20 mg and after several more weeks of cramps and bleeding, the curse finally ended. I was at my wit's end, asking everyone I knew for advice. All my family and friends recommended a hysterectomy and I was ready to do anything but I still had to find an ob/gyn.

It took a couple of months but I finally found a women's clinic that would agree to see me even though I could not pay right away. Our financial situation had not improved and I had applied for Medicaid again which was still pending at that time. I had already been turned down twice for assistance but I stubbornly persisted since we were in such a desperate state. I will not vent my frustrations concerning the denials from Medicaid in this narrative, but the system is not fair. Even with letters from both my hematologist and family doctor and all my medical and financial records showing my need for assistance, I still did not meet their qualifications. Unfortunately I am not a minority or have a bunch of kids and am not at death's door so they did not care.

The group of professionals at Women's Wellness Center understood our situation and agreed to see me and wait until I got an answer from Medicaid before charging me for their services. All through this experience, I have been blessed by finding good caring health providers who are experts and also had a heart.

Dr. Ford had had experience with ITP patients before and ruled out hysterectomy because of the risk with my suppressed immune system and the possibility of infection. Luck had been with me for the past couple of months and I had not had a period during that time so Dr. Ford thought I might be premenopausal. The blood work he had done confirmed that possibility. That was where his services stopped. There was nothing else he could do at that point. If I started bleeding again, there were other procedures such as an ablation or medications we could use that would bring on menopause. All we could do was to wait and see what happened.

****

I was diagnosed at age 15 after noticing I had a lot of nosebleeds and what I learnt were petechiae. My GP sent me for a full blood count and my count was sub 20K, which scared my parents as I have a family history of Leukemia, which was swiftly ruled out. My Doctor took a watch and wait and "no contact sports" approach for a while before starting me on Prednisolone (Prednisone). Being a 16 year old girl in the middle of exams, putting on weight, being unable to play sports, concentrate or control my moods was less than ideal to say the least, and it knocked my confidence. I had very supportive friends and teachers, but in general, kids could be pretty unkind. I was put on a course of Rituxan just before I was 17, which took me out of school for a day every week, and took a lot of explaining when I really didn't want the attention. Happily, it gave me a 2.5 year remission, which let me get through the end of secondary school with a good set of grades. I gained a lot of my confidence back, got to go dancing again and (probably most impressively with funny platelets) I passed my black belt in karate by the time I was 18! I then left home for university; lots of excitement, a whole new world that I absolutely loved! After the end of my 1st year however, I was hospitalized with a count of 3k, completely out of the blue. I've been on and off steroids for the past year, and have tried Immunosuppressants to no avail. I'm currently having another course of Rituxan and hoping for the same result I got first time around. I have a wonderful and supportive family, great friends, my internet support network and a boyfriend who has been more amazing than I could have hoped. Karate is on the back burner for now but I'm back dancing, and have just passed my 2nd year at university with a 1st class grade. I'm focusing on what I can do while fighting ITP instead of what I can't do, I think a positive approach is the best way, though we're all allowed a dark day every so often. I've decided to not let this mad disorder stop me doing what every other young woman my age does- whatever I want, within reason!

Caitlin Jones - Llandudno, Wales, UK

6 WHAT DO WE DO NOW

I want off this rollercoaster! I'm sick and tired of being sick and tired. ITP is like nothing else I have seen, and that's the problem! Nobody can "SEE" it. I keep hearing "you look fine", but if I'm fine why do I feel like crap?

Hap Hapner - Miami, FL

I was a very unhappy person. My platelets were down in the 30s–40s and I felt terrible. My arms and legs were bruising, I was so tired and to top everything off, I started bleeding again. I tried to get back in to see Dr. Ford but the clinic would not work with me on a payment plan. My Medicaid application had been turned down again and I did not have the funds to pay for an office visit. The receptionist that I spoke with said, "Sorry, payment in full at time of visit. I hope someone else can help you."

That ticked me off. It seems, especially in the field of gynecology, that access to medical care is based on finances and controlled by the insurance companies. The general attitude is expressed in a quote from Charles Dickens' *A Christmas Carol*. The Ghost of Christmas Present queries Scrooge, "If Tiny Tim is to die hadn't he best get about it and decrease the surplus population?" This is not to say that all ob/gyns subscribe to this way of thinking, but many do.

Dr. Goldberg was not too pleased with my platelet count being low but did not want me to up my daily dose of Prednisone, but I did anyway. I went to 10 mg a day and also increased the Provera. I had to stop the bleeding somehow or another. It worked, after a month of on and off, light and heavy flow, it stopped.

For the next couple of months, everything was looking up. I was feeling better, my platelets were staying in the 40s, I had no periods, but that short holiday ended when I went in for my monthly CBC and my platelets had dropped to 15,000. Dr. Goldberg expected that to happen eventually and was not surprised; actually he already had another course of action in mind. Since the Prednisone was not doing the job, he wanted to try a stronger steroid called Decadron. I took the maximum monthly dosage of 40 mg each day for four days, during which time I felt terrible. I was either hyper or wiped out, unable to sleep, and very nervous. The reason for the roller coaster ride was that the Decadron was seven times stronger than Prednisone, the daily 40 mg dose was equivalent to 280 mg of Prednisone, but it did the trick. My platelets were up to 78,000 the following week and kept going up to over 100,000. Then they crashed back down to 22,000.

It had been a month since I had taken the first dose of Decadron so we tried another round. Dr. Goldberg also prescribed Ativan to help with the anxiety and sleeping problems. Again I was very sick and had fluid buildup in my cheeks, knees and ankles. Everything tasted terrible and I felt like I was going crazy, but my platelets went up to 151,000 and stayed up for about two or three weeks. Then the bleeding started, slow at first, but over the next couple of weeks, it got worse and worse until one night it turned into a gusher with gigantic clots. I had to change pads every two hours. Could it get any worse?

Yes, that morning I had a fainting spell for the first time in years. About 10 years prior to that, I had been on a very strict diet where I consumed less than 1000 calories a day. I lost weight but when my blood glucose dropped too low, I would get a warm sensation that traveled up my body. When the warmth reached my head, I would lose all muscle control and collapse. It only lasted for a few minutes, but it seemed like a lot longer.

That morning, my muscles turned to rubber and I fell flat in the hallway. I was trying to get to the bedroom before I collapsed but did not quite make it. Somehow I crawled into the bathroom where Bob was shaving and he took charge of the situation. I was sweating profusely; felt slightly disoriented and had trouble talking. The sweating and rubber legs only lasted about five to ten minutes as in previous episodes but the disorientation and slurred speech had not ever happened before. Needless to say, we were both scared to death. Bob wanted to take me straight to the emergency room at the hospital, but I only got as far as the bedroom. I was too weak to walk any farther. The disorientation cleared up following a short rest on top of the bed and everything seemed to be back to normal.

We had already planned to go to another clinic that morning so we proceeded to follow through with that instead of going to the ER. A home health nurse we had been working with suggested we try the walk-in clinic since they have a sliding scale payment policy and was fully set up for women's care. It was just what we were looking for. The only drawback was it was about fifty miles from our home but we were willing to give it a try. We were in desperation mode. After an hour's drive to the clinic, we discovered that none of the doctors was in that day. I was very upset but it was my fault. I had not called ahead since it was a walk-in clinic so the wasted trip could only be blamed on me.

I called the Cancer Center informing them of the situation. Since another month had passed, we started the third round of Decadron and increased the Provera. I suffered from the same side effects as before but worse since losing so much blood. Dr. Goldberg put me back on Slo-FE to build up my hemoglobin, and as before, in less than two weeks, the bleeding stopped and my platelets went up to 186,000, the highest they had ever been since I was diagnosed with ITP.

The following month followed the same routine, minus the bleeding. Even without the bleeding, my platelets dropped to 16,000. I took the Decadron for the fourth time but nothing happened, my platelets did not go up. Dr Goldberg thought that might have been due to a very bad sinus infection I had at the time. He said whenever a person has an infection; the platelet production drops off but not to worry. He had another treatment he wanted to try, another IV drug called Vincristine. We did the Decadron one last time while waiting for all the paperwork to be completed for the new treatment. That was a mistake. My face swelled up and was red and puffy. The bloating was worse than ever, I was very tired and draggy and the worst part, the side effects did not go away after I finished the four-day course.

It got to the point where I could not function at all, no energy or motivation and I could not think straight. I was a wreck emotionally, physically, and psychologically. I honestly thought I was going crazy and was waiting for the men in white coats to come, put me in a straightjacket and take me away. That is the absolute truth; I felt like I was going off the deep end never to return. The worse part was it did not have the desired effect on my platelets, no big jump in the count like with the other treatments. The extreme side effects continued for about three or four days after I had finished the Decadron. I told Dr. Goldberg about my bad experience and he told us it was withdrawal from the drug and we were never going to use Decadron again. Anyway, everything was set up for the Vincristine.

He had some other good news as well. He told us about a new drug, IMG531 that was being tested and thought I might be able to get into the program. I was too late to get into the clinical trials at MUSC (Medical University of South Carolina), but it was being experimented with by a few doctors. The new drug promoted platelet production within the bone marrow instead of suppressing the immune system like steroids do. He set me up with another hematologist, Dr. Raj, to see if I qualified and could try the new medication even though the FDA had not approved it yet.

Even though my platelets were back down to 17,000, everything was looking positive with the first Vincristine treatment, but if fate followed the same routine, something had to happen to pop my balloon. It did; I started bleeding again. I had been off Prednisone while taking the Decadron and had not had any steroids for two weeks. Dr. Goldberg hoped the Vincristine would raise my platelet count sufficiently and as an added measure, I also increased the Provera again.

No luck this time. I was very stressed, could not sleep, eat, relax or stay still, just like I was before going to the hospital the first time and that did not help matters either. The bleeding continued to worsen, especially at night with a very heavy flow and gigantic clots. I started having problems with chest pain, rapid heartbeat, shortness of breath and was very pale and tired. I could barely make one lap around the yard (with several rest stops) walking Tippy.

Bob took me to the Cancer Center where we got good news and bad news. My platelets were up but my hemoglobin was rock bottom, dangerously low. It was January, 2007 and for the third time in a year and half I was admitted into the hospital. I had to spend the next day at the hospital getting transfusions. I had bled so much that I needed three units of blood. It took twelve hours to complete the process, but I could tell right away that it made a difference. The walk to the car afterwards was chest pain free and best of all my period finally stopped a few days later.

The next several months was filled up with doctor appointments. I was seeing Dr. Raj about the experimental platelet drug, consulting with another ob/gyn, along with my weekly trips to the Cancer Center for the Vincristine. Dr. Goldberg decided to give me a week's break between the second and third IV treatment to see if I developed any neuropathy, a side effect from the drug.

We were glad he had the foresight to do so because during that week off, my fingertips went numb and stayed that way for several months, which was devastating at that time. A few months prior to that, I had gotten a job as a freelance reporter for a local newspaper and was at the computer every day writing up my articles. It was very difficult to type with dead fingertips but I stubbornly kept it up, we needed the money. That's the way our luck seemed to go at the time, one step forward, two steps backward.

The doctor told us that we were fortunate that the numbness was just in the fingertips. The neuropathy could have affected my hands and feet if we had gone ahead with the third and fourth treatment and could have been very serious, never fully recovering from the neuropathy. No more Vincristine. Since my platelets were still too low, he put me back on 60 mg of Prednisone even though he did not like it. He was worried about the side effects from prolonged use of the drug such as reduction in bone density and eye problems as well as the suppressed immune system.

The other two doctors were very helpful and did all they could to help me. Dr. Raj researched the experimental platelet-boosting drug and found that it was not available to individual patients who had already gone through a splenectomy so that ruled me out. He made some suggestions to help with my platelets yo-yoing up and down though. He suggested using Prednisone again in a constant low dose, 10-15 mg instead of varying doses, or to get an IVIg every month. I had had an IVIg when I was in the hospital and had no ill effects from it except for a headache. The only problem with that plan was the cost, several thousand dollars a pop. When I had my first relapse, we were going to do an IVIg at the Cancer Center but the cost was prohibitive. The least expensive way to get the IV was to check into the hospital as an outpatient but that was still out of our budget.

The ob/gyn, Dr. Brady, did all the routine tests and decided I needed an ablation to stop my periods. That consisted of a balloon being inserted inside my uterus and filled with hot liquid to cauterize the inside of the uterus to stop the bleeding. Both Dr. Goldberg and Dr. Raj were not too fond of that idea, favoring the use of medication such as Depo-Provera instead. The procedure was too chancy with my suppressed immune system risking any type of infection.

My luck finally began to change. I did not have another period until six months after the transfusion and it was normal. I did not need to use the Depo-Provera even though my family doctor had it on hand just in case. My platelets had remained pretty steady during that time even with a gradual reduction in the Prednisone to 5 mg and I thought everything was looking up. Well, sort of looking up. My vision was getting quite blurry, but after all I was nearly fifty years old. All I needed was some reading glasses, yeah, right.

****

I was born and raised in Illinois just east of St. Louis, Missouri. I was a healthy bull of a man, six feet, 230lbs, broad shoulders with a small beer gut. Not bragging but I was strong as an ox, smart as a whip (stop laughing) and had a great sense of humor with an easy infectious smile. Work was hard, play was even harder and I enjoyed life to the full tilt side of the meter. I turned 50 in August of 2005 and within 2 months my life changed. On Nov 3, my wife made me go to the doctor. I had been having a small steady trickle of blood from my nose, waking up from sleep with a trail of blood from my nose and mouth running down my chin, neck and chest. At the doctor's office a nice young student doctor turned white as a ghost in examining me, finding blood sacks hanging from my blackened mouth. He left the room and returned with a physician's assistant, who in turn left and returned with an MD. The doctor knew what I had quickly; he just had his first ITP case three weeks earlier. A quick trip to the hospital confirmed low platelets with a blood test and I was admitted with a count of 5000. No drugs or treatments had any effect; no change in temp, blood pressure or breathing, nothing. Even my appetite was still good and my sense of humor was on full positive. Within three days they could not detect any platelets. The bone marrow aspiration was and still is the worst pain I have ever endured. I wouldn't wish that on my worst enemy. Yep, I had ITP but positive thinking and attitude was going to beat this crazy thing!!!!!! Nov. 17 was the day they decided that my 2 healthy spleens needed to come out to try to get my counts up. I was released in a few days with

136,000 platelets. Just before Thanksgiving, I noticed my left leg was swollen. They found a clot behind the left knee so back into the hospital. They gave me Heparin for the clot and my counts dropped down to 35. I went into HIT. I had the medical staff rushing around now trying to deal with blood clots and no platelets. I was finally sent home after about 1 week, platelets at 175. My platelet count was bouncing everywhere and prednisone dosages were changing just as fast. Three days before Christmas 2005 my counts were at 10 so off to the hospital for 2 units of platelets. One week later counts at 18, no transfusion because what did I do with the platelets from last week? The prognosis was not good. The doctor told my family to start shopping for a casket; I would probably not make it into the New Year. On Jan 5, I walked into the hematologist's office and received hugs from all the staff. No one had expected me to still be alive. I proved them wrong as to my will. All drugs and treatments stopped since nothing helped my counts, which were at 24. Early Feb I got very sick at work, not flu, just felt like crap, missed several days of work. Blood test on Feb 10 showed count of 136, Feb 26 counts at 237. Work was no problem but had swelling in both legs. I was put on Warfarin due to blood clots behind knees in August 2006. Counts were still high but now I suffered from severe pain in both legs and had to start wearing heavy compression knee high stockings. The whole medical team was scratching their heads. I qualified for full disability in August 2007. I had blood clots in lungs Feb 2008, several more clots behind knees and lympedemia in legs. No one can explain why I am still alive. Numerous and multiple clots in lungs should have put me in the ground. Funny, I built and prepped race cars and boats for many well-known pro drivers, earning several national championships for a highly regarded racing team in a national series (USAC). I slept maybe 4 hours a day, ate the worst diet known to any single man, had a stress filled job and hobbies, was never sick a day in my life, made sure my boat got wet at least twice a week during the season and water-skied. I just loved life and the people in it. Then I got married, turned 50, stopped having way too much enjoyment for one person and botta bing, botta boom, ITP hit me like a...well my life was changed. I am divorced now and trying to regroup, starting over at age 55. Thank GOD for old friends who are trying their best to relight my fire! God must have a plan in store for me. I will do my best as always to be ready for whatever is coming.

Tom Schilling - Greenville, IL

7 THE GIFT OF SIGHT

It's a weird thing, this ITP. Just remember, you have to focus on the things you can do while fighting this mad disorder, not the things you can't.

Caitlin Jones - Llandudno, Wales, UK

I was in heaven, the vaginal bleeding had stopped completely and my platelets were remaining steady on the low dose of medication. I had been totally off the Provera for several months since Dr. Brady had told me it could promote the bleeding to start again.

My work as a freelance writer was going great. I had started out writing for one of the local papers and lucked out on another freelance job writing for a health and wellness supplement in another newspaper that had a larger circulation. I absolutely loved researching and writing on health related topics. I met some really great people and hopefully helped some of the readers understand more about taking care of themselves. I also continued writing on this narrative and on my novel called *Gerald and the Wee People* a fantasy novel designed for young people.

I had also taken on some marketing jobs, maintaining DVD and telephone displays in several stores in the local area. It was not very glamorous work but it did bring in money to pay the backlog of bills. It kept me busy and made me feel like I was contributing to the family finances.

My eyes started giving me some problems. Everything was getting progressively more and more out of focus and it was becoming very difficult to see anything clearly. I bought stronger reading glasses, that helped with my work but I had to stop driving. That was OK too, I hated to drive and I had a chauffeur, Bob.

It was December 2007 and everything was looking good until I had another sudden drop in my platelet count and my arms and legs were covered with bruises. There was no reason for it to happen. I was no longer bleeding but I was down to 5 mg of Prednisone. Dr. Goldberg said that it was just the nature of ITP and upped the Prednisone to 60 mg. He also made an appointment with another hematologist, Dr. Steward, at the Medical University of South Carolina (MUSC) in Charleston, SC. He wanted to try a second time to get me on the new platelet building medication (AMG531) and since they did the clinical trials at MUSC, maybe I would have better luck getting approved. Dr. Goldberg did not like the continued use of Prednisone, especially the higher doses. The side effects were too numerous and could possibly outweigh the benefits.

Dr. Steward was sympathetic with my situation and wanted to help but told us we would have to wait until the AMG531 was approved by the FDA and came on the market. He understood the concern we all had with the Prednisone and suggested another try with the Rituxan. He had had pretty good success with some of his ITP patients using the IV treatment.

Meanwhile, my body had reacted very badly to the increased dosage from 5 mg to 60 mg of Prednisone. I was very antsy, hyper and anxious. I had a panic attack while Christmas shopping in Walmart. Bob and I had split up to do the shopping and I was in the middle of the store when the attack occurred. All the other shoppers seemed to be closing in on me and I had to escape but could not remember in what direction to go to get to the door. I was frozen to the spot in the middle of an aisle and just stood there for who knows how long. The next thing I recall is being in the parking lot looking for the car with a bag in my hand. I must have checked out but the memory still eludes me. Luckily we had parked in one of the end spots and Bob was already in the car. After I stopped shaking and told him of my misadventure, we went straight home.

A part of the disorientation at Walmart was due to my eyes. Cataracts are one of the side effects of Prednisone. My vision had been deteriorating over the past year and with all the other problems I was having, I put off having an eye exam. Six months prior to my panic attack, I had to stop driving because of my poor eyesight and the blurry vision rapidly got worse. Bob had to drive me to do interviews for my articles and also to do my marketing jobs. It got to the point where both my near and distance vision were extremely limited. It was getting very hard to read even with the strongest reading glasses I could buy along with a magnifying glass.

When I had numb fingertips, I jokingly told Bob the only thing worse than having no feeling in my fingers would be to go blind. It was only a joke, but I guess the big guy upstairs took me literally.

Everything I did depended on being able to see. I needed my eyes to do all my chores around the house and with the dogs. Have you ever tried walking an obstinate dog while not knowing exactly where you are going? Tippy was the only dog I had to walk on a leash but that was enough; he had a mind of his own and was stronger than I was. He was OK as long as we stayed on our well-beaten path, until he saw another dog or a cat, rabbit, possum, squirrel or a snake. He hated snakes most of all and took me for several excursions into the woods or into the side of the barn chasing critters.

The worse part of my declining sight was the effect it had on my writing. The newspaper articles helped to pay our ever-increasing monthly bills and I could not give it up. I started using a tape recorder when doing interviews, which was a big help and Bob did the photography. To write up my notes, I used a big fat magic marker on large pieces of paper and set the font on the computer to the biggest print it would type.

It was so frustrating to take a whole day just to complete one article but I was stubborn. Bob helped a lot by proofreading all my work and being very patient with my inability to do all the things I normally did. Along with having to drive me everywhere, he had to lead me across parking lots, help with the shopping, read aloud to me all the things I could not read on my own and so much more. My husband was an angel.

You may wonder why I did not get my eyes fixed before they got so bad; the answer – lack of funds. I was legally blind by the time I found out about the Commission for the Blind. Since my work as a writer depended upon having two good eyes, the Commission accepted my application and agreed to help pay for the surgery on both eyes.

The initial eye exam showed that I had developed cataracts caused by all the Prednisone I had taken over nearly three years' time. Instead of smooth cataracts like most people develop, mine were crystallized and refracted light. That was why my outside vision dropped off faster than my inside vision.

Thanks to the good folks at the Commission for the Blind both of my eyes were fixed. The left one was worse so it was done first. On the way home following the surgery, I drove Bob crazy by reading all the signs and billboards along the side of the road. It was so amazing how well I could see with just one eye done. A month later, the second lens was replaced. Now I had two good eyes, which was absolutely wonderful. I could go back to the way things were before the cataracts got so bad. I could do all my chores with the dogs and around the house. I could write again without having to use a magnifying glass and extra large print. Bob did not have to read everything for me or lead me by the arm whenever we had to walk somewhere. I could drive again.

It was a major adjustment being able to see again, perceptions were different but beautiful. Following is an article that was published in "Vitality" the health and wellness supplement in one of the local newspapers.

The Gift of Sight

By Greta Burroughs

Last week, I sat and gazed at the sunset. It had been a long time since I had witnessed the sight and I did not want to miss a moment of it. The cloud formations and the colors on display above the horizon were spectacular. What an absolutely beautiful experience.

The gift of sight is so often taken for granted until it is lost. Then the simple everyday tasks of reading labels or sending an email or walking the dog become major obstacles. When a person lives in a perpetual fog, unable to see anything clearly, it becomes frustrating not being able to do what used to be second nature.

That is what happened to me. The medication that I take to control my blood disorder called ITP (Idiopathic Thrombocytopenic Purpura) caused life changing side effects. My eyes developed crystalline cataracts and got to the point where I was legally blind.

Thanks to Jan Bunch and the Commission for the Blind, I was able to get my eyes fixed and can now see again. The change was miraculous. Within the space of a few hours, my eyesight went from foggy to clear. The advances made in cataract surgery over the past few years including the development of flexible, foldable lenses are amazing.

On the way home after the surgery, I drove my husband crazy reading all the billboards and signs, pointing out the flowering shrubs and giving a running commentary on everything I saw. I walked our dog the following day and could actually see where he was leading me. We did not have to follow the usual obstacle free path; instead we were free to roam. The only negative aspect of my reacquired vision was seeing how bad a job I had done with the housework.

As a writer, clear vision is a necessity. Prior to the cataract surgery it was a pain, both literally and figuratively, to write. But now that I can see again, there is no more need for magnifying glasses and large font on the computer, no more having to guess where the letters are on the keyboard and no more missed deadlines.

The gift of sight is a wondrous blessing we should all treasure and cherish. Life is filled with beautiful sights and yes; beauty is in the eye of the beholder.

****

The side effects from some of the medications prescribed for ITP are life altering. For me, it was the cataracts caused by Prednisone. The opinion that the treatments are sometimes worse than the disease is very prevalent among the folks that have been treated with steroids. The weight gain, joint pain, bloating, moon face, sleepless nights, gastrointestinal discomfort and mood swings are terrible.

Also, we have to worry about cataracts, osteoporosis, hypertension (high blood pressure), diabetic metabolism (blood sugar changes), delayed wound healing, atrophy (muscle wasting, including the heart muscle), potassium loss, and changes in the skin. The side effects can be devastating and can grow in severity if the treatment is continued for a long period of time. Withdrawal from the drug can also cause problems; hence Prednisone has to be tapered off slowly. Decadron is just as evil to cope with. It is stronger than Prednisone and since there is no tapering-off period, the withdrawal is more than some people can bear. For myself and others I have spoken with, we will never go through the torture of Decadron again.

After having ITP for a while, most of us can tell when our platelets are low, not only by the bruising, petechiae, nose bleeds or mouth blisters, but by the fatigue and depression associated with low platelets. When confronted with how to remedy the problem, most hematologists will opt for increased dosages of Prednisone before trying other treatments but that is usually just a temporary fix. As soon as the dosages are reduced, the platelet count plummets. I have been very fortunate that I have been able to maintain a steady count on 10 mg of Prednisone.

Some ITPers absolutely refuse to take steroids and demand other options such as IVIg or Rituxan. This is the way to go if you have insurance or a payment plan because they are expensive. These treatments have been very successful resulting in remission for many people but then again may not work for others. Everyone is different; what works for one person will not work for another.

ITP was recognized over fifty years ago. It may not be very well known or a top priority to researchers and drug manufacturers but there has to be another first-line treatment that does not destroy our bodies. This concern has been raised by many people suffering with ITP and one of the reasons I am writing this narrative.

Life is hard having an obscure chronic illness that no one understands. An ITPer can look and feel great or be depressed and fatigued. In either case, his/her body has a little war going on inside. It is very frustrating to hear comments like "Well, you don't look sick" or "At least you don't have cancer." Maybe not, but we have an internal problem that has totally screwed up our lives. This is not meant as a slight against our caregivers but it is very difficult for friends and family members to understand the dilemma we face unless they have been through it.

ITP is real. According to the PDSA, this disease affects 9.5 out of every 100,000 adults and 5.3 out of every 100,000 children. Most kids have acute ITP but for the one percent with chronic ITP who cannot run and play without fear of injury, it is the ultimate torture for them and their parents. The parents have the added burden of deciding which treatment is best for their child and then have to watch the kid suffer through it.

Many health providers are not familiar with autoimmune disorders and ITP can be misdiagnosed. This can lead to extreme consequences. One mother posted a comment on the PDSA Facebook page stating that she was very concerned about all the bruises on her nine-year-old daughter and took her child in for a check-up. Instead of doing a medical examination, the doctor reported the mother to Social Services for child abuse. It was not until the mother looked up the symptoms on the internet and went back demanding blood work, was it found the child had a platelet count of 1000.

Education is the key to enlightening the world about this blood disease. More people need to know what this disorder is and how it affects lives. Once more folks are aware, more research will follow that will hopefully find better treatments and one day possibly a cure for ITP.

****

I was on prednisone for 2 1/2 years and as of tomorrow I will be off of them for 3 weeks! Last Tuesday I was at 36 and the doctor wanted me back on them. I said "You spend 2 1/2 yrs on steroids and let me know how you feel," so when my platelets dropped Friday I got the IVIG, I am hoping this will keep them up for a while.

Jessica Wolcson McNally - Long Island, NY

****

Maybe it's ignored because for most people with low platelets it's a symptom of some other disease. For us, it IS the disease. And it's a very well hidden disease. For many of us, we can't feel it and often can't see it. It's easy to forget it's there. When I was an inpatient, the docs came in expecting to see a "sick" person, but were always amazed that I'd already been up, taken a shower, dressed and just chilling out in bed. They were expecting me to look sick. When you don't look or act sick, docs don't think much about it. My platelets were only 10 at the time and I felt great.

Karen Wilson Walker - Durand, MI

8 REMISSION

Hearing high platelets numbers (higher than they were before) is music to our souls...

Yaneth Rognack - Miami, FL

Dance even if it means closing your eyes, listening to the music and picturing yourself dancing.

Jackie Fiamengo-Sunara - San Pedro, CA

June 2011

I had no more relapses following my eye surgery in April 2008 and I celebrated the one-year anniversary of my last period in July 2008. I am officially menopausal, never to be haunted by that curse again but that was the only good thing that happened that year.

After my successful cataract surgery and the beginning of my remission, Mom found out she had a cancerous mass next to her kidney. She was in intense pain and was hospitalized after a botched biopsy caused internal bleeding. She spent the next three months in the hospital and in a nursing facility before passing away.

After my father had passed away in 2006, we kept in contact with Mom by phone but were unable to visit her because of medical or financial complications. I was only able to get up to see her twice because of the difficult times we were having at home. We did not have a reliable vehicle to make the 700-mile round trip and no money to fix our car. Our friend, Silke, flew me up for Mom's birthday and drove me up the second time right before she died. I drove my mother's car back home after the second visit but we had to turn around and go back a few days later for her funeral.

During that same time, our two outside dogs passed away as well. Max was bitten by a copperhead or rattlesnake. We gave him antihistamines and at first he seemed to get better but his thirteen-year-old body could not fight the infection caused by the bacteria the snake injected in him along with the venom. Heidi had spent her whole life with Max and did not understand why he was no longer with her. She stopped eating, drinking water and playing and simply grieved herself to death. The last night she was alive, she wandered all around the inside of the barn looking for Max, finally giving up the search to lie down never to wake up again. We might have been able to save Max and Heidi but did not have the funds to take them to the vet. It was so hard to watch them die and not being able to do anything about it. Our veterinarian had the same policy as the gynecologists we had to deal with, payment in full at time of visit.

Meanwhile Mom was fighting her cancer and we could not be with her to give any comfort. It was a terrible summer and Bob and I both suffered greatly. The stress got to Bob and caused him to have severe palpitations. His doctor made him wear a heart monitor and did a bunch of tests that showed his heart was OK, but we knew why the palpitations were so bad, stress and fast food. After Mom's funeral, when things started to settle down, the pain stopped.

The only good thing that happened that summer of 2008 was that my platelets were behaving. I am glad to be in remission now but I would rather have Dad, Mom, Max and Heidi still with us too. I miss them all dearly. The four of them were all very special and helped us through all our ordeals in their own special ways.

During the last couple of years, my platelets have stayed above 50,000 and even went over 100,000 for several months. I did develop hip problems, which was another side effect of Prednisone. It was very painful especially at night. The slightest movement sent shooting pains from my hip to my calf muscles. The pain was so severe that I could not put any weight on my leg in the mornings. I hopped around until the muscles stretched out and relaxed. We researched the symptoms and determined it was sciatica but then my imagination took over and I convinced myself it was cancer. It's funny how a person's mind can make you believe things even though there is no reason to. I finally broke down and went to my family doctor who agreed with our diagnosis of sciatica but took x-rays of my hip and leg to be sure. What a relief when I was told it was just arthritis, not cancer.

Our Annie was having hip problems too. The old girl could no longer walk without assistance but she never lost her smile. Some people may not believe that dogs have feelings or emotions but they do. She was always happy, even when in great pain. Even when we were saying our good-byes before putting her to sleep, she gave us a big smile and tried to wag her tail. That was a very difficult decision for us to make but her quality of life was not good anymore. Annie could not get around on her own anymore and she could no longer control her bodily functions. We believe she went to be with Max and Heidi to run, play and chase balls for the rest of eternity.

Dr. Goldberg was pleased with my platelet count remaining constant. It did not matter what the numbers were, as long as there were no big fluctuations. He called me his 'miracle girl' and told me to keep on doing whatever it was I was doing. He still did not like my taking so much Prednisone but there was not much else that worked for me. I was on the lowest dose that worked for me, 10 mg and since that is considered to be a safe dosage, we decided to stick with it.

The platelet drug, Nplate (formally known as AMG531) that we tried to get on when I was having so many relapses was finally approved by the FDA. Recent research had shown that many people with ITP also have a platelet production problem in the bone marrow. Nplate had been approved for the treatment of ITP in this category. The Cancer Center set me up in a patient assistance program through Amgen, the drug manufacturer for weekly shots if my platelets bottomed out again.

Luckily, I never needed it and was not sure if we would have gone that route even if I had needed it. Dr. Goldberg had had mixed results with other patients that tried Nplate and was concerned about the possible bone marrow problems it could cause. Also, no one knew what the long-term side effects would be since it was brand new.

When I wanted to be a guinea pig during the clinical studies, I was desperate enough not to care about side effects. Now that that I am in remission, we feel no great need to take any chances. We are comfortable with Prednisone as long as we can keep it down to 10 mg.

Since I was originally diagnosed with ITP, some significant events have take place in my life. First of all, I did not realize how close I came to dying at the beginning of this saga until after I had gotten out of the hospital and on the computer. The Scripps website that I mentioned earlier gave a detailed description of ITP and I also had a chance to learn more about platelets. Bob and I realized that considering how fast the platelet count decreased from 8000 to 2000 in a matter of hours that fateful Friday, if I had not requested blood work the day before, we would never had known the severity of my condition. I probably would have died that weekend with neither of us ever knowing why.

The second close encounter occurred when I had another unending period and wound up in the hospital for three units of blood. The chest pain, fatigue and breathing problems that sent us to Dr. Goldberg's office for a CBC was my body's way of saying, "I'm running out of blood, do something NOW, stupid!"

All the relapses had a negative effect on everyone involved; not only me and Bob but also the good folks at the Cancer Center and our friends and family. My parents were extremely concerned and worried every time they got any bad news. They were having a very rough time with their own cancers but still called almost every day to see how I was doing. We were not able to spend the time with my folks that we wanted to and that was hard on all of us.

Bob has been my anchor. Without his help and support, I do not know if I could have handled all my relapses and other problems. We have been and still are a team. When I have needed him, he was always there. When he had medical problems, I tried to give him the same consideration and love.

Another source of support I recently found was the PDSA (Platelet Disorder Support Association) Facebook page. Oh, how I wish it had been available six years ago when I was first diagnosed with ITP. Bob, Dr. Goldberg, my friends and family have been absolutely great during this ordeal but to actually communicate with fellow ITPers makes a big difference in how I view this chronic blood disorder.

I have spoken with women who have been through the same type of bleeding problem I had and found out I am not alone. There are some ladies that are now facing the same dilemma and I feel useful being able to explain what I did and hopefully help someone in need with my advice.

Many of the people on the PDSA Facebook page are going through Rituxan, Decadron, Vincristine or Nplate treatments and ask about the side effects and results from the folks that have been there, done that. It is amazing how the same treatments can have such varied results.

Comments are made about good news and bad news. The good is cheered on by well-wishers and the bad is made a little bit better by messages of support and reminders to keep a positive attitude. The mental, emotional and psychological toll on any person suffering with an incurable disease can be very devastating no matter what the age. Parents want to know how to help their children. Teenagers have a very difficult time not being able to participate in sports and other activities with their friends. One high school student found out in a very hard and painful way who her true friends really were. Young adults are cut down in their prime child bearing/rearing years. Middle-aged and older adults wonder if the treatments are worse than the disease.

This group of people I have come to know and respect are more like an extended international family. There are no political or racial differences ever noticed. Religious beliefs may vary but both 'Allah bless you' and 'God bless you' are said with the same genuine concern. Many have commented that there are no other ITP patients where they live and the ability to talk and share with others makes life a little less complicated. Several of my fellow ITPers contributed comments and stories, which I have included in this book.

The Facebook page is an offshoot of the PDSA website http://www.pdsa.org, the best site I have found for all things ITP. The Platelet Disorder Support Association is dedicated to enhancing the lives of people with immune thrombocytopenia (ITP) and other platelet disorders through education, advocacy and research. It is the nation's leading non-profit health organization dedicated to supporting adults, children and families with

ITP. This organization is devoted to bringing you the most timely, accurate and comprehensive information about ITP. They also promote research to find promising therapies and ultimately a cure for ITP and other platelet disorders. I strongly encourage everyone to check out their website or call toll free: 1- 87-PLATELET (877) 528-3538.

Our future looks bright as long as both of us stay healthy. We are both happy with our writing careers. Bob has published two novels, *Riders of the Wind* and *Winds of Fate* and is working on two more books. I have published *Gerald and the Wee People* and have some other books underway as well.

We still have three of our four-legged children. Unfortunately, Tippy is no longer with us and Spike and Baby are getting up in years; both of them are slowing down and sleep most of the time. Another puppy wandered into our yard recently and never left. Lil'bit is a Basenji mix full of vim, vigor and vitality. She keeps us on our toes and entertains us with her silly antics.

I am in remission. For how long, who knows, but I am glad to still be here to tell you my story. Hope you enjoyed. Thank you.

****

I've had ITP since 2008, and I'm surprised at how many people in my area who have never heard of ITP. I went into remission for a year and a half, and then had it recur this past April. This time around I have made it a point to find others who are going through this same thing. That's when I found PDSA and others close by as well. I have been keeping a journal and am amazed when I look back at the things I have been through. I have had the opportunity to speak at several local churches about my experience and continue to do so. There is not very much about ITP out there and to me that's sad. So many diseases get media attention and yet there is so little known about a disease that is just as cruel. I think it is time people were educated about ITP. I agree wholeheartedly about learning all you can - ask questions, be persistent. My hematologist told me a few weeks ago that I knew more about ITP than most doctors do. I told him I better, I live with it everyday!!!

Emily Frey McTyre - Rockmart, GA

****

The only thing that is consistent is that we all react differently. Remission just means that counts have been "normal" for an extended period of time. Since ITP is idiopathic, there is no clear explanation for what triggers it, or when or if a relapse occurs. The bad news is that a relapse can come at any time. The good news is that there is always hope that remission can also come at any time. Even though there are a lot of doctors out there that don't know much about ITP, there are also a lot of really smart people out there looking for answers / treatments / cures. And even though relapse can happen at any time, the treatments of tomorrow will be better than the treatments of yesterday. It is important for patients to have patience, and stay positive.

Keith Hart - Stillwater, MN

ABOUT THE AUTHOR

While working her way through college, Greta Burroughs taught in a developmental center for handicapped and delayed preschoolers. That is where she developed her love of reading to children and also first started creating her own stories.

After marrying Robert Burroughs, Greta devoted her time to working with her husband in the field of aviation. Robert was a Federal Aviation Administration (FAA) designated pilot examiner while Greta maintained the office and administered FAA written tests. Even during that busy period in her life, she did not lose her love of reading or writing.

After both of them experienced serious medical issues which took them out of professional aviation, Robert and Greta began new careers as writers. Robert published two novels in his exciting Riders of the Wind series while Greta worked as a freelance reporter for a local newspaper. In her spare time, Greta worked on a series of children's picture books entitled *Patchwork Dog and Calico Cat* and a young adult fantasy novel, *Gerald and the Wee People*. She also kept a journal of her experiences while being treated for a chronic blood disorder called ITP. The treatments, relapses and remissions along with the information she found out about ITP was compiled into a book entitled *Heartaches and Miracles*.

Robert and Greta reside in South Carolina with their four-legged children keeping busy at their computers creating articles and books to share with others. They both have plans for more books and will continue writing as long as they possibly can.

OTHER BOOKS BY GRETA BURROUGHS

Gerald and the Wee People (a young adult fiction/fantasy novel)

Two teenagers respond to a plea for help and literally fall into another world. They become involved in a war and invent some clever plans to temporarily prevent the enemy from entering the village of the wee people. Time is running out, the gates are getting weaker and the weapon stash is dwindling. Something else has to be done to stop the war.

Gerald, Vernon and six companions embark on a quest to defeat the crazed forest god who is set on destroying all the inhabitants living on that world. They follow a path described in an old prophecy but things do not go as planned.

House on Bo-Kay Lane (book two in the Wee People series; will be available in summer, 2012)

Gerald and Vernon believe their time with the wee people came to an end after they returned to their home world but begin to wonder when strange things started to happen at an abandoned house in their neighborhood. Ghostly images of familiar faces are seen in the windows, echoes of voices from the past haunt the boys' dreams and an undeniable curiosity draws Gerald and Vernon to investigate the mysterious haunted house. What they find takes them back to the world of the wee people and a new adventure begins.

Patchwork Dog and Calico Cat (a book for beginning readers; will be available in winter 2011)

Patchwork Dog has a knack for getting into trouble and his best friend, Calico Cat usually winds up right in the middle of the mess with him. Join the two curious creatures as Patchy tries to unsuccessfully fly like a bird and gets caught nosing around an airplane. Together they eat too many apples, confront a not too friendly skunk, and take a magical ride into town. The five stories will entertain beginning readers with the antics of the title characters and hopefully teach youngsters some valuable lessons on sharing and working together.

RECOMMENDED READING

Riders of the Wind by Robert F. DeBurgh

Winds of Fate by Robert F. DeBurgh

Riders of the Wind, the first novel in DeBurgh's series takes you along on a grand adventure with Charlie and Doretta Cross and their friends during the pioneering days in aviation of the late 1920's until the beginning of World War II. The reader will experience the golden age of aviation including the great air races, rum running, the birth of the airlines, exploration in the jungles of Brazil and much more. This novel is filled with romance, adventure, humor, sadness and mysticism, something for every reader.

Winds of Fate continues the Cross' story during the World War II years. It takes the reader from the security of the civilian airlines to Natal, Brazil, across the South Atlantic to India and the heroic Hump operation over the Himalayas. It also takes the reader through the world of the WASPs and the lives of the female ferry pilots who flew military airplanes within the United States under the most difficult conditions.

Made in the USA
San Bernardino, CA
15 March 2014